APPROACHES TO GOD

APPROACHES TO God

JACQUES MARITAIN

FOREWORD BY
JOHN G. TRAPANI, JR.

Paulist Press
New York / Mahwah, NJ

Copyright © 1954 The Jacques Maritain Center
Translated by Peter O'Reilly, first published by Harper & Brothers, 1954
This edition published in 2015 by Paulist Press. Foreword copyright © 2014 by
John G. Trapani, Jr.

Cover image by vovan/Shutterstock.com
Cover and book design by Lynn Else

Library of Congress Cataloging-in-Publication Data

Maritain, Jacques, 1882-1973.
    [Approches de Dieu. English]
    Approaches to God / Jacques Maritain ; foreword by John G. Trapani, Jr.
        pages cm
    ISBN 978-0-8091-4833-2 (pbk. : alk. paper) — ISBN 978-1-58768-242-1
(ebook)
    1. God (Christianity)—Knowableness. I. Title.
    BT101.M42953 2015
    231`.042—dc23

                                                                2014038031

ISBN 978-0-8091-4833-2 (paperback)
ISBN 978-1-58768-242-1 (e-book)

Published by Paulist Press
997 Macarthur Boulevard
Mahwah, New Jersey 07430

www.paulistpress.com

Printed and bound in the United States of America

CONTENTS

FOREWORD

John G. Trapani, Jr., PhD

PAST PRESIDENT, AMERICAN MARITAIN ASSOCIATION
PROFESSOR OF PHILOSOPHY, WALSH UNIVERSITY

"There is not just one way to God....For man, there are as many ways of approach to God as there are wanderings on the earth or paths to his own heart." These words, taken from Jacques Maritain's Preface to his book, *Approaches to God*, in many ways set the stage for what readers will encounter in his concise yet insightful book. As a man who is perhaps the foremost spokesperson for the philosophy of St. Thomas Aquinas in the twentieth century, Jacques Maritain is also a formidable and original thinker in his own right. For this reason, readers of this book (originally published in Paris in 1953; English translation, 1954) should not be surprised to discover that, in addition to his lengthy commentary on Aquinas's classic five proofs for the existence of God, Maritain also offers valuable insights and new philosophical arguments concerning approaches to God that go beyond the cogent reasoning of Aquinas.

The *division* of Maritain's book is easy enough to see when one takes even a casual glance at the table of contents; the *understanding* of Maritain's book, however, may not be as simple. This is especially true for those who are not conversant with Thomist philosophy. Accordingly, this foreword has two sections. In the first section, I discuss the division of the topics in Maritain's book. By grasping the structure of his book and surveying its philosophical topology, so to speak, readers will have a realistic assessment about what to expect from these pages...and what not to expect. Moreover, for those who do not wish to engage this book by reading from cover to cover, this topic tour also serves to direct readers to those chapters where they will find their desired material of interest.

Depending upon readers' philosophical sophistication, especially their familiarity with the Thomist tradition, the second section of this foreword may prove more valuable. In it, I first discuss several key ideas that are central to the Thomist conceptual framework, especially in metaphysics. Secondly, I discuss a few essential concepts that are unique to Maritain's own philosophical thinking. Although Maritain's expansion of certain Thomistic terms and concepts is consistent with Aquinas's thought, having a clearer understanding of the unique meaning of some of Maritain's key ideas will help readers to appreciate the richness of his thought. And finally, I also offer a few comments about Maritain the writer; after having read Maritain for over forty-five years, my simple suggestions may serve to enhance one's comprehension and enjoyment of his books.

SECTION ONE:
THE DIVISION OF MARITAIN'S
APPROACHES TO GOD

In chapter 1, Maritain begins by discussing a primordial or pre-philosophical approach to God. While this approach depends upon the natural intellectual character of human nature, it does not employ any carefully developed logical reasoning. Rather, central to Maritain's approach is his unique use of the notion of "intuition," a term that he inherited from his first teacher/mentor, Henri Bergson. Although his use of it is uniquely his own, it nonetheless rests solidly within the Thomist (and not Bergsonian) philosophical tradition.[1]

Since Maritain's comprehensive understanding of human nature undergirds all of the many humanly possible approaches to God that he identifies, in the second chapter, Maritain moves from the use of our intellect in a primordial or pre-philosophical way to the properly philosophical reasoning about God. Drawing upon the fundamental distinction between the speculative and practical intellect, this chapter shows the speculative intellect operating at its finest level of philosophical reasoning. Maritain's lengthy analysis begins by commenting on the value and validity of Thomas's five arguments in general. Then, by adapting Aquinas's own method, he next articulates some of the possible new objections that modern thought, especially in the natural and experimental sciences, has raised, and he concludes by carefully responding to each of those objections. Since many people tend to read Aquinas's proofs on a superficial level (and thus misinterpret them), Maritain's general comments help those interested in a more serious and more correct understanding of these proofs, even as he leads them to a deeper appreciation of each in its philosophical profundity. Chapter 2 is the longest chapter in the book and perhaps the most intellectually rigorous.

Maritain the original thinker shines forth in chapter 3. If Aquinas's five ways proceed from observations of change and motion in the physical world, Maritain's "sixth way" begins with an introspective analysis of the intellect's own activities. While remaining within the speculative operation of the intellect, Maritain astutely guides us to reflect upon our own intimate experiences of the very nature of the intellect itself. By doing this, Maritain's new sixth way calls attention to the fact that, while our bodies may be physical and hence corruptible, the intellect itself is spiritual and hence incorruptible. Since our spiritual nature can only originate from a spiritual Creator, in this way, Maritain offers a novel and legitimate, even if ethereal and somewhat difficult, affirmation of God's existence.

In chapter 4, "The Ways of the Practical Intellect," Maritain discusses those approaches to God that come from either the conceptual or the non-conceptual "connatural" activity of the Practical Intellect. Although none of these approaches possess the logical force of the rational arguments in the strict sense of the word, Maritain maintains that these approaches to God are powerful and have their own validity nonetheless. Specifically, this chapter discusses three of these approaches from the practical intellect.

They are: (1) those that occur through the poetic experience of creativity and aesthetic beauty; (2) those that occur through the ethical experience of true moral goodness; and, (3) those that occur through the theological experience and witness of those whose saintly lives confound, enrich, and inspire us.

Maritain's concluding chapter 5, "The Desire to See God," takes up a serious discussion that proceeds from the limits of purely rational, properly philosophical thought and brings us to the very beginnings of theology and, by extension, to the doorstep of mysticism as well. Whether we are consciously aware of this or not, our human nature, specifically our spiritual intellect and will, *naturally* desires the "supernatural" (God). The truth is, however, that the "purely natural" alone can never satisfy this desire. And yet, as Maritain explains (following St. Thomas): just because it is not *necessary* that our natural longing and desire be satisfied, the spiritual nature of our desire points to something beyond the purely natural and this leads to the conclusion that the natural longing of our desire has at least the *possibility* of being satisfied. Here we move to the beginning of theology since this natural desire truly can only be satisfied when we are "elevated to the life of faith" through the gift that God gives of himself. Thus, we learn of the possibility of our obtaining a knowledge of God that is superior to reason, a mystical knowledge that occurs when we see God as he is in himself, "face to face."

Since much of the book is Maritain's commentary on the wisdom of Aquinas concerning the approaches of human intelligence to God, Maritain prudently concludes his book with an appendix that contains, without comments, selected passages from Thomas's *Summa Theologica*. These are the texts upon which Maritain has commented in his book and their inclusion will be especially appreciated by those who want to read St. Thomas for themselves without having to seek out these passages elsewhere. Discussion groups also will find this material helpful.

SECTION TWO:
SOME AIDS TO UNDERSTANDING MARITAIN'S
APPROACHES TO GOD

There are three Thomist metaphysical terms that Maritain employs and that are especially important for understanding Thomas's Five Ways: (1) the role of analogy in thinking about being or existence; (2) the distinction between existence and subsistence; and, (3) the distinction between essence (*essentia*) and existence (*esse*).

Concerning the first, the reader will do well to keep in mind that things may be said to "to be" or "to exist" in many ways. As examples, we might say that angels exist, antelopes exist, Superman exists, beauty, truth, and goodness exist, and that colors exist. While all of these things *exist*, we can see that they do not all exist *in the same way*: angels exist as purely spiritual beings, antelopes exist as physical beings, Superman exists primarily as a creative idea (a being of the mind), while beauty, truth, and goodness, are transcendentals and as such, they cut across all metaphysical categories. Reflecting on this basic fact helps us to see two things: first, that the terms being or existence are not univocal terms, and second, that analogical thinking—the idea that terms may be predicated of things in ways that are the same and yet different—is essential for metaphysical thinking.

When we contrast these examples with the final example above, colors, we are led to a consideration of the second essential distinction. Since colors are qualitative modifications of those things that possess color, they are traditionally called "accidental qualities" or "accidents." By contrast, angels and antelopes, since they have their being or existence in themselves, are called substances. Substances *subsist*,[2] while accidents, since they do not have their existence in and of themselves, are said to exist *in another*; that is, while they *exist*, they do not *subsist*.

By combining the insights from these two basic distinctions (existence and subsistence, and the analogy of being), we then come to the third and final vital distinction. While subsistent things, substances, all have the fact of their existence in common, *what* they are (i.e., the kinds of beings they are) differs. The terminology that accounts for the whatness of a substance is called its essence (*essentia*), and from the fact that an actually existing substance *is*, we are able to account for the "*is-ness*" of a substance, that is, its existence (*esse*) or, what is more properly referred to as, its "act-of-existing."

Although Maritain presumes that his readers are familiar with this terminology, we know that this is surely not always the case, and so the comprehension of these three distinctions is important since it enhances our understanding of Aquinas's Five Ways. This is especially true when Aquinas or Maritain refers to God as either (1) the *Ipsum Esse Subsistens*—best translated as the Self-Subsisting Act-of-Existing—or as (2) that being whose Essence *IS* His Existence (Act-of-Existing). By understanding this latter distinction, we also are led to a deeper and richer appreciation of the depth of meaning contained in the answer that God gives to Moses when asked for his name: "I Am Who Am." God is that being whose very essence is "the act-of-existing" and as such, he is the act of all acts and the perfection of all perfections, since existence is the ultimate perfection. For this reason, we also understand God as the First Cause precisely because he also is First Act. This insight is especially enlightening when we keep in mind that the term "First" refers to a metaphysical, and not chronological, priority.

As mentioned, Maritain, the twentieth-century Thomist philosopher, also brings his own unique contributions to the traditional Thomist vocabulary. First of all and foundationally, his philosophy places particular emphasis on the unique attributes of the human person, especially on those that follow from the uniqueness of the human spiritual intellect. Maritain's insights in this regard are especially important since they bring to light aspects of human nature which, due to the contributions of centuries of advances in science and scientific knowledge, Aquinas, in his own day, did not, and indeed could not, do. While emphasizing the organic unity of the person, Maritain stresses that, although our sense powers serve the intellectual powers, it is of the nature of the intellect to permeate all of our senses and their various forms of intuition.[3] For Maritain, as for St. Thomas, our being in the "image and likeness of God" derives specifically from the unique spiritual nature of our intellect and will; it is through the activity of these spiritual powers that we are able to know God and to love him.

Another term that requires special attention concerns what Maritain calls "the intuition of being." Not mediated by any concept, for Maritain the intuition of being enables the intellect to have an immediate insight into the actuating influx of God's creative power *ex nihilo*. Maritain refers to a form of this intellectual intuition in every chapter of his book. Should one fail to grasp the full meaning of Maritain's understanding of human nature, the human spiritual intellect (especially intuition of being), and the interrelation of all of our cognitive powers, one would fail to understand and appreciate the depth of insight that Maritain has contributed to the conversation about the approaches to God found in this little gem of a book.

And finally, a word about Maritain the writer: on the one hand, Maritain's writing style is often complex, dense, and somewhat obscure, especially when he writes within the strict framework of technical Thomist terminology. His sentences are often long and sometimes convoluted. My suggestions for reading him in this regard are two-fold: first, read slowly and pay attention to all punctuation as you do so; punctuation may serve as stylistic road signs, as it were, that may help readers to navigate some conceptually rugged terrain. Second, readers will often be rewarded if they read aloud. The mental insertion of these additional pauses and punctuation may well serve to enhance comprehension. On other occasions, however, and sometimes when we might least expect it, Maritain's writing will be completely down-to-earth and filled with common sense examples that help to make otherwise difficult passages perfectly clear.

But make no mistake: Maritain the writer is also part poet and part mystic. And so, beyond the aridity of his technical philosophical writing or his sometimes folksy practicality, Maritain also frequently surprises and delights his readers with flashes of great poetic beauty, of profoundly simple wisdom, and of grand, lofty and elegant prose graced with bolts of spiritual brilliance that inspire and delight, even as they offer us glimpses of the ineffable here on this very earth. For Catholic readers looking for greater understanding of the essential complementarity between their reason and their faith, Jacques Maritain leads the company of those gifted few who lighten and brighten us on this most sacred of journeys, namely, the pursuit of those "many ways of approach to God" that are as diverse, abundant, and luminous as the many paths to the human heart itself.

NOTES

1. Maritain's meaning of the term *intuition* will be discussed further in section two of this foreword.

2. There are three categories of substances: elements, compounds, and all living beings.

3. For a wonderful explanation of Maritain's unity and interrelation of all of the human knowing powers, see his, *Creative Intuition in Art and Poetry* (New York: Pantheon Books, 1953), chap. 4, 106–11. For a discussion of the many varied types and uses of the words *intuition* and *connaturality*, see my treatment (and charts) in *Poetry, Beauty, and Contemplation: The Complete Aesthetics of Jacques Maritain* (Washington, DC: Catholic University of America Press, 2011), especially chapter 3.

PREFACE

He is inaccessible yet he is close at hand. He encompasses man on all sides. There is not just one way to God, as there is to an oasis across the desert or to a new mathematical idea across the breadth of the science of number. For man there are as many ways of approach to God as there are wanderings on the earth or paths to his own heart.

I have tried in this little book to mark out some of these ways: those, to wit, which from the point of view of philosophical reflection would seem to be the principal ones. My readers will excuse me for having taken up again here and there views expressed in previous essays. It is the grouping of these diverse approaches in an articulated whole which, it seems to me, gives interest—if it has any—to the present work.

Here it is a question only of that knowledge of God that we can attain by reason or by the natural forces of our mind. For what concerns the knowledge of God brought by faith and by the gifts on which mystical experience depends, we refer the reader to the excellent little book by Charles Journet, *The Dark Knowledge of God,*[1] and to our work, *Les Degrés du Savoir.*

NOTES

1. A translation by James F. Anderson (London: Sheed & Ward, 1948), of the original French work, *Connaissance et Inconnaissance de Dieu* (Paris: Luf, 1943). On the rational proofs of the existence of God, see the fundamental work of Father Garrigou-Lagrange, *God, His Existence and His Nature* (St. Louis, MO: Herder, 1939), a translation by Dom Bede Rose from

of every man, philosopher or not. It is this doubly *natural* knowledge of God I wish to take up here. It is natural not only in the sense that it belongs to the rational order rather than to the supernatural order of faith, but also in the sense that it is *pre-philosophic* and proceeds by the natural or, so to speak, instinctive manner proper to the first apperceptions of the intellect prior to every philosophical or scientifically rationalized elaboration.

Before entering into the sphere of completely formed and articulated knowledge, in particular the sphere of metaphysical knowledge, the human mind is indeed capable of a pre-philosophical knowledge that is *virtually metaphysical*. Therein is found the first, the primordial way of approach through which men became aware of the existence of God.

2. Here everything depends on the natural intuition of being—on the intuition of that act of existing which is the act of every act and the perfection of every perfection, in which all the intelligible structures of reality have their definitive actuation, and which overflows in activity in every being and in the intercommunication of all beings.

Let us rouse ourselves, let us stop living in dreams or in the magic of images and formulas, of words, of signs and practical symbols. Once a man has been awakened to the reality of existence and of his own existence, when he has really perceived that formidable, sometimes elating, sometimes sickening or maddening fact *I exist*, he is henceforth possessed by the intuition of being and the implications it bears with it.

Precisely speaking, this primordial intuition is both the intuition of *my* existence and of the existence of things, but first and foremost of the existence of *things*. When it takes place, I suddenly realize that a given entity—man, mountain or tree—exists and exercises this sovereign activity *to be* in its own way, in an independence of *me* which is total, totally self-assertive and totally implacable. And at the same time I realize that *I* also exist, but as thrown back into my loneliness and frailty by this other existence by which things assert themselves and in which I have positively no part, to which I am exactly as naught. And no doubt, in face of my existence others have the same feeling of being frail and threatened. As for me, confronted with others, it is my own existence that I feel to be fragile and menaced, exposed to destruction and death. Thus the primordial intuition of being is the intuition of the solidity and inexorability of existence; and, second, of the death and nothingness to which *my* existence is liable. And third, in the same flash of intuition, which is but my becoming aware of the intelligible value of being, I realize that this solid and inexorable existence, perceived in anything what-soever, implies—I do not yet know in what form, perhaps in the things themselves, perhaps separately from them—some absolute, irrefragable existence, completely free from nothing-ness and death. These three leaps—by which the intellect moves first to actual existence as asserting itself independently of me; and then from this sheer objective existence to my own threat-ened existence; and finally from my existence spoiled with noth-ingness to absolute existence—are achieved within the same unique intuition, which philosophers would explain as the intu-itive perception of the essentially analogical content of the first concept, the concept of Being.[2]

Next—this is the second stage—a prompt, spontaneous rea-soning, as natural as this intuition (and as a matter of fact more or less involved in it), immediately springs forth as the necessary fruit of such a primordial apperception, and as enforced by and under its light. It is a reasoning without words, which cannot be expressed in articulate fashion without sacrificing its vital con-centration and the rapidity with which it takes place. I see first that my being is liable to death; and second, that it is dependent on the totality of nature, on the universal whole of which I am a part. I see that Being-with-nothingness, such as my own being, implies, in order that it should be, Being-without-nothingness—that absolute existence that I confusedly perceived from the beginning as involved in my primordial intuition of existence. But then the universal whole of which I am a part is itself Being-with-nothingness, by the very fact that I am part of it. And from this it follows finally that since this universal whole does not exist by virtue of itself, it must be that Being-without-nothingness exists apart from it. There is another Whole—a separate one—another Being, transcendent and self-sufficient and unknown in itself and activating all beings, which is Being-without-nothing-ness, that is, self-subsisting Being, Being existing through itself.

Thus, the internal dynamism of the intuition of existence, or of the intelligible value of Being, causes me to see that absolute existence or Being-without-nothingness transcends the totality of nature. And there I am, confronted with the existence of God.

3. This is not a new approach to God; it is human reason's eternal way of approaching God. What is new is the manner in which the modern mind has become aware of the simplicity and liberating power, of the natural and in some way intuitive character, of this eternal approach. The science of the ancients was steeped in philosophy. Their scientific imagery was a pseudo-ontological imagery. Consequently, there was a kind of continuum between their knowledge of the physical world and their knowledge of God. This latter knowledge was seen as the summit of the former, a summit that had to be scaled by the multiple paths of the causal connections at work in the sublunar world and the celestial spheres. And the sense of Being, which everywhere and always ruled their thought, was for them an atmosphere too habitual to be regarded as a surprising gift. At the same time, the natural intuition of existence was so strong in them that their proofs of God could take the form of the most conceptualized and the most rationalized scientific demonstrations, and be offered as a skillful unfolding of logical necessities, without losing the inner energy of that intuition. This logical machinery was surreptitiously enlivened by the deep-seated intuition of Being.

We are in quite a different position now. In order to reach physical reality in its own enigmatic way and to conquer the world of phenomena, our science has become a kind of *Maya*—a Maya that succeeds and makes us masters of nature. But the sense of Being is absent from it. Thus when we come to experience the impact of Being upon our mind, it appears to us as a kind of intellectual revelation, and we become keenly aware both of its awakening and liberating power, and of the fact that it involves a knowledge separate from the sphere of knowledge peculiar to our science. At the same time we realize that the knowledge of God, before being developed in logical and perfectly conceptualized demonstrations, is first and foremost a natural fruit of the intuition of existence, and that it imposes itself upon our mind through the imperative force of this intuition.

In other words, we have become aware of the fact that in its primordial vitality the movement of the human reason in its approach to God is neither a pure intuition (which would be suprahuman), nor the kind of philosophical reasoning of a technical type through which it will be expressed in its achieved form, and which at each of its stages is pregnant with conflicts and with problems to clarify. In its primordial vitality the movement of the human reason in its approach to God is a *natural* reasoning, that is, intuitive-like or irresistibly maintained in, and vitalized by, the intellectual flash of the intuition of existence. In this natural reasoning it is just this intuition of existence which, seizing in some existing reality Being-with-nothingness, by the same stroke makes the mind grasp the necessity of Being-without-nothingness. And nowhere is there any problem involved, because the illumining power of this intuition takes possession of the mind and obliges it to see, in such a way that the mind proceeds naturally, within a primordial intuitive flash, from imperative certainty to imperative certainty. I believe that from Descartes to Kierkegaard the effort of modern thought—to the extent that it has not completely repudiated metaphysics and if it is cleansed of the irrationalism which has gradually corrupted it—tends to such an awareness of the specific *naturalness* of man's knowledge of God, definitely more profound than any scientifically developed logical process, and an awareness of the primordial and simple intuitiveness in which this knowledge originates.[3]

4. I have just tried to describe the manner in which this natural prephilosophic knowledge spontaneously proceeds. It involves a reasoning, but a reasoning after the fashion of an intuitive grasp, bathed in the primordial intuition of existence. Let us say that this natural knowledge is a kind of *innocent* knowledge, a knowledge

free of all dialectic. Such a knowledge is rich in certitude, a certitude that is indeed compelling, although it exists in an imperfect logical state. It has not yet crossed the threshold of *scientific* demonstration, whose certitude is critical and implies that the difficulties inherent in the question have been surmounted through a scrutiny of the rational connections and necessities involved. Such natural knowledge is still in happy ignorance of these difficulties and of all the *videtur quod nons*: because scientific certitude and the objections to be met—and the replies to the objections —all come into the world together.

It appears, therefore, that the philosophic proofs of the existence of God, let us say the five ways of Thomas Aquinas, are a development and an unfolding of this natural knowledge, raised to the level of scientific discussion and scientific certitude. And they normally presuppose his natural knowledge, not with regard to the logical structure of the demonstration, but with regard to the existential condition of the thinking subject. If the preceding observations are true, it would be necessary, before proposing the philosophic proofs, to be assured insofar as possible (by trying, where need be, to aid in such an awakening) that the minds to which one addresses oneself are alive to the primordial intuition of existence, and conscious of the natural knowledge of God involved in this intuition.

One more remark seems to be called for here. I have just used the expression "the philosophic proofs of the existence of God," and I noted above that St. Thomas Aquinas preferred to use the word *ways*. He had his reasons for this.[4] These ways are proofs, but the words *proof* or *demonstration* may be misunderstood. To prove or to demonstrate is, in everyday usage, to render evident that which of itself was not evident. Now, on the one hand, God is not *rendered evident* by us. He does not receive from us and from our arguments an evidence that he would have lacked. For the existence of God, which is not immediately evident *for us*, is immediately evident *in itself*—more evident in itself than the principle of identity, since it is infinitely more than a predicate contained in the notion of a subject. It is the subject, the divine essence itself (but to know this from immediate evidence, it would be necessary to see God). On the other hand, what our arguments render evident for us is not God himself, but the testimony of him contained in his vestiges, his signs, or his "mirrors" here below. Our arguments do not give us evidence of the divine existence itself or of the act of existing which is in God and which is God himself—as if one could have the evidence of his existence without having that of his essence. They give us only evidence of the fact that the divine existence must be affirmed, or of the truth of the attribution of the predicate to the subject in the assertion "God exists."[5]

In short, what we prove when we prove the existence of God is something that infinitely surpasses us—us and our ideas and our proofs. "To demonstrate the existence of God is not to submit him to our grapplings, nor to define him, nor to take possession of him, nor to handle anything else than ideas that are feeble indeed with regard to such an object, nor to judge anything but our own radical dependence. The procedure by which reason demonstrates that God is places reason itself in an attitude of natural adoration and of intelligent admiration."[6] And thus the words *proof* and *demonstration*, in reference to the existence of God, must be understood (and in fact are so understood spontaneously) with resonances other than in the current usage—in a sense no less strong as to their rational efficacy but more modest in that which concerns us and more reverential in that which concerns the object. On this condition, it remains perfectly legitimate to use them. It is just a matter of marking well the differences in station. This being understood, we shall not hesitate to say "proof" or "demonstration" as well as "way," for all these words are synonymous in the sense we have just specified.

As to the very word *existence*, the existentialist philosophers arbitrarily corrupt its meaning when they say that to exist is "to stand outside oneself."[7] But even in its genuine meaning—to stand "outside its causes" or "outside nothingness" (the etymological sense of the word being *"sistere ex,* that is to say, to stand or to be posited in itself, from an anterior term on which it depends"[8])—the word *existence*, in order to apply to God, must lose the connotation which thus refers it to created things. It is clear that God does not stand "outside his causes"—as though he were caused; nor "outside nothingness"—as though nothingness preceded God; and that he is not *sistens ex*—as if he depended on some antecedently existing source. Of itself, however, the notion of existence is in no wise restricted to such a connotation, which in fact refers to the analogue that falls first and immediately under our apprehension; from the outset it overflows all pseudo-definitions carried over from this connotation. Just as the notion of being, the notion of existence is of itself, essentially and from the first, an analogous notion, validly applicable to the uncreated as to the created. No doubt, the word *being*, in contrast to the word *existence*, does not need to be purified of accidental vestiges due to etymology. Truth to tell, however, the word *existence* has been spontaneously purified of them, all by itself, and in any event this does not affect at all the meaning itself of the notion. Those who think that one can say "God is," but not "God exists," maintain for being its essential analogicity but refuse it to existence—the strangest of illusions, since being itself is understood only in relation to existence. To say "God is" and "God exists" is to say exactly the same thing. One speaks the language of simple truth in speaking of the ways through which it is shown that God is, or that he *exists*.

NOTES

1. For a discussion of the ontological argument and of the primacy unduly attributed by Kant to this argument, see our *Dream of Descartes* (New York: Philosophical Library, 1944), chap. 4.

2. On the concept of Being, see our book *Existence and the Existent* (New York, Pantheon, 1948), chap. 1.

3. The preceding pages (2–5) are adapted and reprinted from Jacques Maritain, *The Range of Reason* (New York: Scribner, 1952), 88–90.

4. See *Les Degrés du Savoir* (Paris: Desclée De Brouwer), 445–446.

5. See *De Potentia*, q. 7, a.2, ad 1; *Summa Theologica*, I, 3, 4, ad 2; *Les Degrés du Savoir*, 837–839. It is regrettable that for want of having seen this very simple distinction, theologians such as Dr. Paul Tillich, one of the most remarkable representatives of Protestant thought in the United States, believe that to wish to demonstrate the existence of God is to deny it. (See Paul Tillich, *Systematic Theology* [Chicago: University of Chicago Press, 1951], 204–205.)

6. *Les Degrés du Savoir*, 446.

7. See *Existence and the Existent*, 12, n3; Michel Sora, *Du Dialogue Intérieur* (Paris: Gallimard, 1947), 30.

8. Etienne Gilson, *L'Etre et l'Essence* (Paris: Vrin, 1948), 249.

CHAPTER 2

PHILOSOPHICAL KNOWLEDGE OF GOD

The Five Ways of St. Thomas

5. The five ways of St. Thomas are philosophical proofs. In the perspective of such philosophic systems as Skepticism, Nominalism, Empiricism, Kantianism, Idealism, Pragmatism, Positivism, Dialectical Materialism or Existentialism, their demonstrative value fails to be grasped. Does this mean that they are not valid except in the perspective of a particular philosophy, namely of Aristotelian philosophy rethought and renewed by Thomas Aquinas?

Certainly not. On the one hand, from the point of view of the history and sociology of ideas, it is true that the diverse schools that I have just mentioned represent great philosophies proposed to the world by great thinkers and sometimes by geniuses. Nevertheless, rigorously speaking, it must be said that, from the objective point of view of the intrinsic nature of the diverse types of knowledge, neither Skepticism, nor Nominalism, nor Empiricism, nor Kantianism, nor Idealism, nor Pragmatism, nor Positivism, nor Dialectical Materialism nor Existentialism crosses the threshold at which philosophic knowledge starts. From the beginning—and notably in that crucial domain that is the critical reflection on knowledge and in which philosophical wisdom becomes aware of its proper roots—these systems categorically reject certain primordial truths and original apperceptions that support the noetic structure of philosophical knowledge as such. They are self-destructive philosophies; they punish themselves like the *Heautontimorumenos* of Terence, because by reason of a defect in their primary assertions they have rendered themselves incapable of arriving at philosophic existence. And, naturally, they are not aware of it. They speak much and they say a lot of remarkable things, but they are still in a prenatal state.

On the other hand, in order to recognize in the philosophic proofs of the existence of God, notably in the five ways of St. Thomas, their full demonstrative value, it is not necessary to be a philosopher trained in the school of Aristotle and Thomas Aquinas, or even to be a philosopher by profession. What is prerequisite is to perceive and adhere firmly to the primary truths that Thomist philosophy attempts more successfully than any other to justify—so at least I think. But in the East as in the West, it is by no means the only philosophy to recognize and to cultivate these primary truths. Indeed, the very fact of their primacy prevents them from being the monopoly of any one system; they precede every system. They are part and parcel of what has been called the natural philosophy of the human intelligence (the original ironic use of this expression does not prevent it from being right in itself). They are grasped by common sense before being the object of philosophic consideration.

The philosophical proofs of the existence of God are not established and justified philosophically except at the proper level of philosophy, but they are already valid and efficacious at the level of that philosophy improperly so called—inchoate and spontaneous, incapable of defining its own limits and of criticizing itself—which is the confused knowledge worked out by common sense. Moreover, when a man who is not a professional philosopher hears them expounded with the rigor proper to philosophy, he will but grasp them better and with a certitude, if not more profound, at least more precise and clear—the operation of his intellect being then fortified by its contact with a knowledge of a superior type, which he does not master, it is true, but which he understands (for philosophy does not speak just to philosophers; a wisdom, it speaks also to men). This is how the matter stands precisely because, as we remarked in the preceding chapter, the philosophical proofs of the existence of God are like a decisive unfolding or development, on the level of "scientific" or "perfect" rational knowledge, of the natural pre-philosophic knowledge implied in the primitive intuition of the act of being; and because, on a level much more profound than that of the confused and inchoate "philosophy" of common sense, this root knowledge, even when it is not yet explicitly awakened, is still present in us in a state of unconscious tension and virtuality.

6. What is it, then, that a philosopher ought to know so as to be in condition to grasp on the level of critical reflection the demonstrative value of the philosophical proofs of God's existence?

He ought to know that intellect differs from sense by nature, not just by degree; that what it is looking for in things is Being; and that Being is, to one degree or another, intelligible or attainable by the intellect (otherwise, only fools would philosophize).

He ought to know that the being of things is not one and the same in all things, but differs in each, while being grasped in the same idea of Being and expressed by the same word (this is what Thomists call the analogy of being and of the transcendentals, that is, of the objects of thought that overflow every genus and every category); and that, in regions into which the experience of the senses cannot lead us, the being of things that cannot be seen or touched is nevertheless knowable to the human intellect (which, of course, first set out from experience), *not*, indeed, as if our ideas grasped it immediately, but rather because certain of our ideas, by reason of their very object, pass beyond experience and reach things that are invisible through the relation that unites them to things visible—the relation of likeness that things unseen bear to the world of visible things. (It is this that Thomists call knowledge by analogy.)

He ought to know that the laws of being have as broad an extension as being itself: thus the principle of identity—every being is what it is—is valid over the whole extent of being, absolutely speaking, and the principle of causality holds for the whole extent of being that envelops, in any degree, contingency or mutability. He ought to know that the principle of causality—everything that is contingent has a cause, or again everything that is, without having in itself the whole reason of its intelligibility, is by that token intelligible through another thing—is neither the expression of a simple mental habit acquired as the result of observing empirical sequences and thus bearing on functional connections between phenomena, nor, as Kant would have it, a "synthetic *a priori* judgment" whose necessity follows upon the structure of our mind and whose range is limited to the world of experience. The principle of causality is a principle "known of itself," known by an immediate intellectual intuition that imposes itself upon the mind by virtue of the intrinsic evidence of the objects conceived,[1] and reaches beyond the world of experience, because the "causes" that it asks for are the *raisons d'être*—not necessarily enclosed in the world of experience, any more than being itself is—demanded by things insofar as their *being* is *contingent*.

One sometimes wonders if the five ways of Thomas Aquinas are but different aspects of one and the same proof or if they constitute five specifically distinct proofs. In my opinion, the proper reply to this question is that the nerve of the proof, the formal principle of the demonstration, is the same in each of the five ways, to wit, the necessity of a cause which is pure Act or Being, itself subsistent in its own right. From this point of view, one could say that they form but one proof presented under different modes or aspects. But that which makes a proof is in reality not its formal principle alone, but also its point of departure and the basis on which it rests. And because the proofs of St. Thomas rest on the facts of experience ("philosophic facts"[2]), and because these facts are typically distinct data discerned in the world of experience, it is necessary to say purely and simply that the five ways of Thomas Aquinas[3] constitute specifically distinct proofs.

7. *The First Way: By Motion.* Our world is the world of becoming. There is no fact more indubitable and more universal than motion or change. What is change? This grain of wheat is not yet that which it is going to become; it *can* be what it will become, and when the change is accomplished it will *actually* be that. To

change is (for a thing already "in act," but also "in potency" in other respects) to pass from being in potency to being in act.

But how could a thing give to itself what it does not have? In respect to what it merely *can* be but at present *is* not, it is impossible that it make itself become what as yet it is not. It is something belonging to the order of what is already in act, to wit, the physicochemical energies of the environment, which make the grain of wheat pass from that which it is in potency to that which it will be in act. Everything that moves is moved by another. (Everything that passes from indetermination to determination does so under the action of something else.)

And now, what about the thing already in act, the thing whose action causes another thing to change? Is *it*, itself, subject to change? Does it, in acting, become something more than it was as simply existing? If so, then it is because it is moved to act by another thing. And this latter in its turn, is it moved to act by another agent? Imagine all the agents we please! So long as the agent, from whose action the action of the other agents in the series is suspended, itself passes from potency to act, it is necessary to posit another agent that moves it.

But if there were not a First Agent, the reason for the action of all the others would never be posited in existence; nothing would move anything. One cannot regress from agent to agent without end; it is necessary to stop at a First Agent. And because it is first, it is not itself moved; it is exempt from all becoming, separate from every change and from every possibility of change. It is the absolutely immovable Agent who activates or moves all the rest.

7A.—a) Suppose someone should say that everything changes but without tending toward an end; and that accordingly, change is not a transition from potency to act, but a pure flux of becoming in which there is neither being in potency nor being in act to consider. What then?

First of all, it is not true that everything changes but without tending toward an end. Every change that proceeds from nature is oriented toward an end. But even if the assertion I am denying were true, whatever changes would still pass from potency to act—to an endless series or flux of new determinations, each of which, as it happens in continuous change, is in imperfect act (in act under one aspect and in potency under another), I mean *is going to be*, *is*, and *has been* there in reality, but cannot be isolated from the others save by the mind. It causes the thing that changes *to be in act* in a passing and transient way, but it is *distinct* only *in potency* from the other determinations that continually succeed one another.

b) Suppose one should say that in the atom the electrons that turn around the nucleus are in motion without being moved by another thing. What is to be said in reply to that?

If, for modern physics, matter and energy are but two aspects of one and the same reality—if, in other words, from the moment that you have matter, it follows that by that very fact you have motion—it remains true that matter and energy do not exist of themselves (*a se*) or uncausedly (otherwise they would be God). The cause of movement, then, is to be sought in the cause that conserves or maintains matter in being.

More precisely, it is relevant to note that in speaking of "matter" (or "mass") and "energy," and in saying that matter can be transformed into energy and energy into matter, physics is by no means referring to what the philosopher calls the "substance" of material things—which substance, considered in itself (abstracting from its "accidents") is purely intelligible and cannot be perceived by the senses nor by means of any instrument of observation and of measure. Matter and energy, as understood by physics, are physicomathematical entities constructed by the mind in order to express the real. They correspond symbolically to what the philosopher calls the "proper accidents" or the structural properties of material substance ("quantity" and "qualities"). What we can say, then, from the standpoint of philosophical or ontological knowledge, is that corporeal substance, considered in such or such an element of the periodic table (and disclosed to us only symbolically under the aspect of the "atom" of the physicist), possesses, in virtue of its proper accidents or structural properties, a certain organization in space (which is disclosed to us only symbolically under the traits of the system of electrons, protons, neutrons, etc., of the physicist) and a specific activity which derives from its very essence (and which is disclosed to us only symbolically as the "energy" wrapped up in the system in question). This *natural activity* of corporeal substance appears to the philosophic imagination working on the data of science in the form of an action that the particles composing the atom exert on each other, and on which the movement of the electrons around the nucleus depends. But it is no more uncaused than the being or substance from which it proceeds. This natural activity itself supposes the motion or activation by which the First Cause, running through the whole swarm of activities in the cosmos, causes the production of beings—the ones by the others—in the cycle of the evolution of species, and maintains all natures in existence and in action.

Let it be added parenthetically that this natural activity of matter does not constitute an *immanent* activity such as that of life. Although it manifests the nature of the corporeal substance in dynamic terms through an action exerted by one part on another within the atom, it does not raise the substance from which it emanates from one degree of ontological perfection to a higher one. This raising of itself by itself to a higher ontological perfection by an action emanating from the subject and terminating in the subject itself is the property of life.

c) Suppose one should say that the property of living beings is to move themselves, and that the axiom "Everything which moves is moved by another" is therefore inexact. What reply can be made?

The property of the living is to move itself. True! But it is not by virtue of that in it which is *in potency* that a living being moves itself or causes itself to pass from potency into act, but rather by virtue of its already being *in act* in some other respect. It is not by reason of the fact that a muscle is in potency to contract that it actually contracts (i.e., passes from potency to act), but rather by virtue of something else, to wit, the influx of energy from an *actually* energized neuron. It is not the mere potency of my will in respect to such and such a means that causes my will to pass from potency to act in respect to the choice of that means, but something else, to wit, my *actual* volition in respect to the end. Thus, the axiom "Everything that moves is moved by another" holds in the domain of life as well as in that of inanimate matter. (Moreover, a living being, to the extent that there is potency or mutability in it, is in a condition in which it cannot be entirely self-sufficient. It moves itself, but under the action of other factors or energies in the cosmos. The sun activates or "moves" the vegetal to move itself. The object that impresses the senses incites the intellect to move itself, and the object grasped by the intellect incites the will to move itself.)

d) Suppose someone should say that the principle of inertia, which, since Galileo, is one of the fundamental principles or postulates of mechanics, gives the lie to the axiom "Everything that moves is moved by another." Can this assertion stand?

The ancients had much trouble explaining the movement of projectiles, which, they thought, could not continue in space except in virtue of a certain constantly renewed impulse. According to the science inherited from Galileo (and, before him, from the Parisian doctors of the fourteenth century), local motion, like rest, is a *state*, and a body in motion would continue indefinitely to move with the same velocity if the resistance of the environment did not prevent it.

Is it possible that the progress of modern physics or the requirements of a sound philosophy of nature engaged in a general reinterpretation of the data of science will one day call in question the validity of the principle of inertia?[4] A discussion of the validity of this principle is in any case not pertinent to our present concern. Taking the principle of inertia as established, and even hypothetically granting it a meaning beyond the mere empiriological analysis of phenomena, it suffices, in order to reply to the objection, to note that, applied to movement in space, the axiom "Everything that moves is moved by another" ought then logically, by the very fact that motion is considered a state, to be understood as meaning "Every body that undergoes a

18

change *in regard to its state of rest or of motion* changes under the action of another thing." And thus the axiom remains always true. According to the principle of inertia in its classic form a body once set in motion continues of itself to be moved in a uniform manner or with the same velocity.[5] If then the velocity of its motion increases or diminishes, it will be because of an action exerted on it by another thing. We are thus confronted anew with the axiom, "Every change is produced by the agency of something *other* than the thing that changes, insofar as it changes." And we are obliged anew to ask the question: "Is that something other itself moved?" In this case it is moved, or applied to activity, by another thing.

e) One last question may be posed, namely, on the subject of the Aristotelian principle: *anankè stênai*, it is necessary to come to a stop when one rises from cause to cause. We shall discuss this question apropos of the second way.

8. *The Second Way: By Efficient Causes.* Having considered that *effect* which is everywhere open to our observation, namely change, let us now turn to *causes* and connections between causes. It is a fact, and this is also absolutely general, that there are efficient causes at work in the world, and that these causes are linked to each other or form series in which they are subordinated to one another. Examples always convey to philosophical reasoning a touch of dowdiness, as it were. They are nevertheless necessary. At a bindery one binds a book because the printers have first set it—because the editor has prepared the copy to hand over to them—because a typist has copied the manuscript—and because the author has written the manuscript. A plumcot is used in an advertisement by the commercial artist of a publicity firm because Luther Burbank succeeded one day in crossing the plum tree and the apricot tree and because a book of Darwin on plant variations first aroused Burbank to take up his research. This bee would not visit this rose today if the rose bushes were not in bloom in summer—if the rhythm of vegetal life were not controlled by the diversity of the seasons—and if the revolution of the

earth around the sun, the inclination of the ecliptic being what it is, did not produce the diversity of the seasons. Carnivorous animals live on flesh because there are other animals that live on plants—because plants produce carbohydrates—and because chlorophyll fixes the carbon from the air under the action of light.

Thus, while it is impossible for a thing to be the efficient cause of itself (since it would have to precede its own existence), efficient causes are connected by being complementary to each other, or, in however many varied ways, are conditioned and caused by one another. And this interdependence among causes spreads out in all directions.

It is not possible, however, to go on to infinity from cause to cause. Whatever constellations of causes one may consider apart from the rest within the universal interaction of causes, broaden the field as you will—if there were not a First Cause over and above them on which all the others depend, then all those other causes simply would not be, since they would never have been caused either to be or to act.

It is necessary then to recognize the existence of an uncaused First Cause that exists immutably of itself, above all the particular causes and all their connections.

8A.—a) If it is said that Aristotle's principle, "One cannot go on to infinity in the series of causes," is questionable and does not necessitate the mind's assent, because neither the idea of an infinite multitude nor that of a succession without beginning or end, implies contradiction, this is the answer:

It is perfectly true that neither the idea of an infinite multitude nor that of a succession without beginning or end implies contradiction. But the principle *anankè stênai* neither signifies that no infinite multitude could exist, nor that it is necessary to come to a stop at a first cause in time. The "ways" of St. Thomas do not necessarily conclude to a First Cause in time; rather, they lead to a First Cause in being, in the intelligible conditions of things, and in the very exercise of causality.

There is no contradiction or impossibility in supposing a merely successive infinite series of causes and events succeeding one another in time. There is no contradiction, for instance, in supposing a time without beginning or end, in the course of which living beings beget other living beings without beginning or end. In such a case, if one has to stop, it is only because one gets tired counting. This kind of series is what might be called a "horizontal" series of *homogeneous* causes or causes *on the same level*, each of which merely accounts for the positing of the following one in *existence*.

But the causes to which the principle we are discussing refers do not merely succeed one another in time (whether there be succession in time or not is accidental, for after all, intelligible connections are of themselves nontemporal). They are logically superordinated to one another and one completes the other in the order of the very *raison d'être* or intelligible conditioning. While going back from one to the other in the past, we also rise in being or intelligible conditioning. In other words, these are *heterogeneous* causes or causes *on different levels*. They follow, so to speak, an oblique line; each one, in a certain measure, accounts for the *nature—*or *determination in being—of the action* of the following one.

Accordingly, in regard to them, the principle *anankè stênai* holds with absolute necessity. This is so not by reason of their succession in time, but by reason of the fact that together they set up a particular line of intelligibility or of reasons for existence to which each contributes something, and which cannot be posited unless it depends upon a term beyond which it is impossible to posit any complement of intelligibility; that is to say, unless beyond all particular lines of intelligibility, it is appendent to the "intelligibility-through-itself" of a First Cause, which exists in its own right.

Finally, it is clear that not only the being, but also the action of all other causes, or the causality itself that they exercise, depend at every moment on that First Cause (since it is the supreme reason for all the rest). If then we consider the relation of any efficient cause whatever to the First Cause, we see that this efficient cause would not act at any moment at all if, at that very moment, it were not activated by the First Cause. Every relation

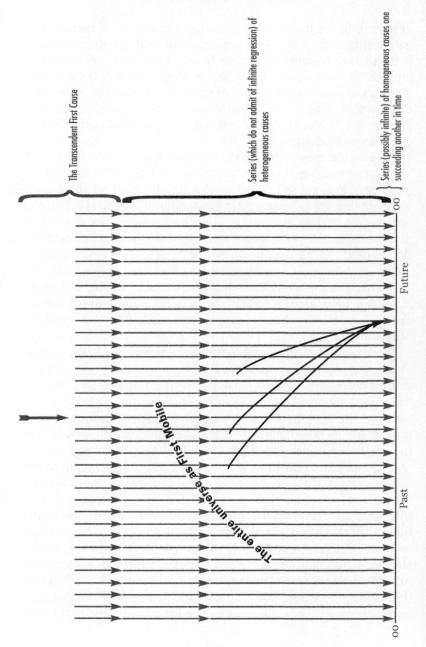

The Transcendent First Cause

Series (which do not admit of infinite regression) of heterogeneous causes

Series (possibly infinite) of homogeneous causes one succeeding another in time

The entire universe as First Mobile

Future

Past

of succession in time in the exercise of causality is here eliminated; the causality of the First Cause embraces and dominates without succession the whole succession of time; it is at each moment the ultimate foundation of the *exercise of the causality* of all the agents that act at that same moment in the world. In other words the line of intelligible conditioning or of reason for existence is, so to speak, "vertical," and leads to a cause that is not only heterogeneous, or on a different level, but transcendent or "separate," infinitely different in nature.

By proceeding from the fact of change and from the fact that efficient causes are connected to the First Cause by way of superordination, we effect a transition to the infinite. This is quite the opposite of a logical movement passing to the infinite from cause to cause (it is rather a logical movement that passes to an Infinite Cause), and it is possible by reason of the analogical character of being.

Immediately below the First Immobile Mover, Aristotle posited a First Mobile, under which the series of subordinate causes was arranged. But in truth, there is no First Mobile, because the First Cause is not first *in* a series, but *beyond* every series. It is the entire universe, with all the natures and clusters of causes dependent upon these natures, which is the "first mobile" in relation to the transcendent First Cause.

b) I said above that neither the idea of an infinite multitude[6] nor that of a succession without beginning or end involved contradiction, and that it is not logically impossible to suppose for example a time without beginning or end in the course of which living beings would have begotten other living beings without beginning or end. It is necessary to understand here, in the first place, that such a time without beginning or end would remain essentially different from *eternity* properly so called, which is also without beginning or end but which is *tota simul*, without any shadow of succession or change—the duration proper to the pure Act in its infinite transcendence. In dealing with the hypothesis of the "eternity of the world," the word *eternity* is to be understood in an equivocal sense, which has nothing to do with true eternity but refers only to a time without beginning or end. In the second place, an always-existing-world would remain strictly a world created *ex nihilo*. For the notion of creation is absolutely independent of that of a beginning in time. A *created* being is one that is caused according to the totality of its being, without any pre-existent matter.

According to St. Thomas' teaching,[7] the fact that the world had a beginning is an article of faith, not a demonstrable conclusion; indeed an event, which is something singular and contingent, cannot be demonstrated by reasons which, since they are drawn from the intelligible structure of things, bear on the universal and necessary. On the other hand, reason cannot establish an event such as the beginning of the world and of time by the procedures proper to historical verification, that are based on the testimony of facts produced in the world and in time.

It might be held that modern science inclines philosophy to regard it as probable that the world (which philosophy knows to be *created*) actually had a *first beginning*; for, without ceasing to be *science* in order to become *history*, science has adopted within the scope of its knowledge the dimension of historical development and thinks of the world as an expanding universe, evolving from a primitive state and subject to a kind of aging process (a striking symbol of which is the law of the increase of entropy). At any rate, the imaginative framework offered by modern science is much more favorable to this idea of a first beginning of the world than was the fixed universe of Greek science. However, what remains essential from the standpoint of philosophy and in the order of assertions of reason is only the strictly demonstrable certitude that the world is *created*: even if it had *always* existed, it would *always* have been caused in the totality of its being, by the transcendent First Cause; in other words it would have been created, or brought into existence *ex nihilo*.

9. *The Third Way: By the Contingent and the Necessary*. Although there is chance in the world (that is, events resulting from the meeting of independent casual series), the indeterminism of modern physics, valuable as it may be on the scientific level, cannot be built

up into a philosophical theory. All happenings in the physical world are determined. This, however, does not prevent their being at the same time contingent to one degree or another. If the proximate causes that produce them had been impeded by the intervention of other causal lines in their particular field of action, or if, in the last analysis, the universe were other than it is, they might not have been produced.[8] In a general way a thing is contingent when its nonoccurrence or its not being posited in existence is not an impossibility. This definition can be verified of a thing taken in itself (a star is no more necessary in itself than a glint of light on a stream), even if it is not verified of the thing considered in relation to the causes that produce it (the stars have been produced as a *de facto* necessary result of cosmic evolution). Change implies contingency. A clear sky becomes clouded; being clear or being clouded are for the sky things whose nonoccurrence is possible. Plants and animals, stars and atoms are subject to the universal rhythm of destruction and production; all the forms our eyes perceive are perishable; they can cease to be. In other words they possess existence in a contingent way.

Is there, however, nothing *but* the contingent, nothing *but* what is *able not to be*? Can we by thought eliminate *absolutely all necessity* from things? The hypothesis destroys itself: on the supposition of *pure contingency*, nothing at all would exist.

Imagine a time without beginning or end; imagine that there was nevertheless absolutely nothing necessary, either in time or above time: It is then impossible that there *always* was being, for that for which there is *no necessity* cannot have been *always*. It is inevitable then that at a certain moment nothing would have existed. But "if for one moment there be nothing, there will be nothing eternally,"[9] for nothing can come into existence except through something already existing. And therefore, right now nothing would be existing.

There must be, then, something necessary in things. For example, matter, understood as the common substratum of all that is subject to destruction and production, must be itself necessary in its permanence through all changes. There must be necessary laws in nature. In other words, things cannot be contingent absolutely or in all respects; they must contain intelligible structures or natures necessarily demanding certain effects.

The question now arises regarding whatever may be necessary in the world of things, whether it derives its necessity from no other thing, or, in other terms, whether it is necessary through itself (*per se*) or in essence (*per essentiam*).[10] In the latter case, there would be neither change nor contingency in things. For what is necessary *in essence* excludes every kind of contingency and change, and exists of itself with the infinite plenitude of being, since, by definition, it cannot be necessary in one respect only.

But if the necessary in things is not necessary *per se* and in essence, in other words if the necessity of the necessary in things is caused, you can imagine all the causes you wish, each of which, in turn, is itself caused, and it will nevertheless be necessary to stop at a First Cause that accounts for all the necessary there is in things, and whose necessity is not caused, that is to say, a First Cause that is necessary through itself and in essence, in the infinite transcendence of the very act of existence subsisting by itself.

9A.—a) Should it be said that the argument is not demonstrative because, supposing that there is absolutely nothing necessary, either in time or above time, one does not have to adopt the hypothesis of an infinite time, but may assume a time finite as to the past; and consequently the argument would not stand because it would be possible that the moment at which nothing would be had not *yet* arrived. The answer is clear.

As an objection this is null and void. For on the hypothesis of a time finite as to the past, the argument bears, as a matter of fact, on the very origin of this time. In fact there would not by hypothesis be any being *chronologically prior* to this time (since it *did* begin). Further, there would not be any being preceding this time by a *priority of nature*, because only a being that is necessary at least in some respect can precede time by a priority of nature, and because it was supposed, in any case, that there is absolutely nothing necessary either beyond time or in time. There would be then *no being* to make the first thing and the first instant at which the time in question presumably began to come into existence.

b) Should it be further alleged that the principle "That for which there is no necessity cannot always be" (*quod possibile est non esse, quandoque non est*) is not self-evident, but only an empirical generalization devoid of intrinsic evidence, what is to be answered?

This principle is in no wise a mere empirical generalization. It is for the intellect an intrinsically obvious principle. It is evident in virtue of the very principle of "reason-for-being" (*raison d'être*). Either a thing is by reason of itself—then it is its own reason; or it is by reason of something else—then it has its reason for being in something else. Correspondingly, a thing is *always* either by reason of itself or by reason of something else. The fact that it never ceases to be has itself a reason. If it is of itself the total reason for its *always* being, then it is necessary by reason of itself. If the reason for its *always* being is something other than itself, then that reason, by the very fact that it guarantees its never ceasing to be, endows it with some kind of necessity.

As noted above, contingent things that do exist in the real world and with which we have to deal always imply a certain bit of necessity, under one aspect or another. They are not the pure contingent. The force of Thomas Aquinas's line of argument comes from the fact that it considers with full metaphysical rigor the hypothesis of the *pure contingent*. In the light of this consideration, it becomes obvious that this hypothesis is not tenable. To posit the pure contingent is to imply that nothing exists.

10. *The Fourth Way: By the Degrees That Are in Things.* It is a fact that there is a qualitative "more or less," that there are degrees of value or perfection in things. There are degrees in the beauty of things (Plato saw this better than anyone); degrees in their goodness; in fine, things *are* to a greater or lesser degree. Knowledge is more highly and more perfectly knowledge in intelligence than in sense; life is more highly and more perfectly life in

the free and thinking living thing than in the animal living thing, and in the animal living thing than in the vegetative living thing.

But wherever there exist degrees (wherever there is a *more* and a *less*) it is necessary that there exist, somewhere, a supreme degree or a maximum (a *most*). I am putting this forward as an axiom, the meaning of which is analogical and admits of typically different realizations. This supreme degree may be either (1) the peak *of the totality* of a progressive finite ensemble of values, or (2) the peak of *one* arbitrarily designated *part* in a progressive infinite ensemble of values, or (3) a peak of infinite value beyond and above the totality of a progressive infinite ensemble (take, for example—although there is no question here of qualitative values—a transfinite number of a power higher than such or such an infinite series).

Since goodness, beauty, life, knowledge, love, and ultimately Being are in things in diverse degrees, it is necessary that there exist somewhere a maximum or a supreme degree of these values.

But the progressive or ascending ensemble of the values in question, inasmuch as they can exist in things, is an infinite ensemble, in which consequently there is no actually supreme degree. One thing is good and another is better, but there can always be another still better. In other words, goodness exceeds or transcends every category of beings, and is not in its fullness in any one of them. Each good or beautiful thing is beautiful or good partially or by participation. It is not, then, unto itself the reason for its goodness. For *that* it would be necessary that it be good *by reason of itself* or *in essence* (then it would have goodness in all its plenitude. But such is not the case). Therefore, it derives its goodness from another thing; it is caused in goodness.

But whatever cause be considered, if it is itself caused in goodness, it derives its goodness from something else. Here again it is necessary to come to a stop at a First Cause which is good in essence and by reason of itself.

In other words, it is necessary that there exist somewhere a maximum or a supreme degree of goodness (and of the other transcendental values of which we spoke).[11] But this maximum or

28

supreme degree, because it is the First Cause of all that there is of goodness in things, is a peak beyond the infinite series of all possible degrees of goodness in things. It is a supreme degree beyond the whole series. It is a transcendent First Cause that is good by reason of itself, which, therefore, does not *have* goodness but *is* goodness—it is Goodness that subsists by reason of itself.

10A.—a) If it be said that the principle "Wherever there are degrees it is necessary that there exist somewhere a maximum or a supreme degree" is but an extrapolation of common experience and possesses neither intrinsic evidence nor universality, we shall reply as follows.

This principle is self-evident inasmuch as it expresses in an entirely general way the logical requirements of the concept of comparative relation. The proposition "Every series composed of a *more* and a *less* connotes a *most*" is a necessary and self-evident proposition."[12] It is verified, as we indicated, in an analogical way and according to typically different modes. It is only if one confuses it with the particular application most familiar to us (the case of a finite progressive ensemble—in a house of many stories there is necessarily a top story) that one can contest its supra-empirical and unconditional universality and necessity.

b) Should it be said that in virtue of this same principle it would be necessary to declare that there is, as ancient physics believed, a supremely hot element (fire), the cause of all the heat there is in nature; further, that there is something supremely solid, the cause of all there is of solidity in bodies; something supremely red, cause of all there is of red in things; and other equally untenable assertions of the same sort—there is a good answer to that.

The objection rests on the same confusion that we have just pointed out. Without doubt, there is as a matter of fact in nature (this is, however, irrelevant to any scientific explanation) a star whose temperature is the highest, a bird whose plumage is the reddest, a body whose resistance is the hardest. But there would be no point in looking in any such order of things for a being which, presumably, would possess the quality in question *per se* or by virtue of its very essence and would therefore be the cause of that quality in other things, for the reason that these qualities, being generic qualities and not transcendental modes of being, do not exist in things *by participation*[13] (except in regard to the transcendent First Cause, which possesses in a virtual-eminent manner everything there is of being or of perfection in the quality in question). This order of things is the domain of univocity, and of beings, values, or perfections confined within genera and categories.

The whole force of the demonstration comes from the fact that it deals with transcendental values or perfections, which surpass every genus and every category, and by their very nature demand existence on ever higher levels of being.

They are analogical, and exist in things by participation, without at any moment being in any subject, however exalted it may be, according to the plenitude of their intelligible content.

Things, as we have seen, hold these values of perfections, which exist in them, from a cause other than themselves, and therefore a cause must ultimately be posited—a cause above the infinite series of all the possible degrees in things—which possesses *through itself* those values or perfections. In that cause, these values and perfections exist in perfect unity, in a *formal-eminent* mode, within the infinite transcendence of the Being per se.

c) Thus the fourth way is concerned with any *analogical* and *transcendental* value or perfection possessed by things. Note, to conclude the discussion of this way, that among these values is found truth: not only ontological truth (or the truth of things), which is identical with being, but also logical truth (or the truth of the knowing intellect), insofar as it is a perfection of the intellect and is shared by intellects to more or less elevated degrees. A mere factual truth (it is raining this morning) is less elevated in the scale of truth than a scientific truth such as the law of falling bodies. So physical truths are less elevated in the scale of truth than either mathematical truths or metaphysical truths, both of which are eternal, that is to say that their object is beyond time. The idea of number is drawn from sense experience, but once it has been disengaged by the intellect, it places the intellect itself in the presence of an objective world, a world that exists, no doubt, only in the mind, but that nevertheless exists as a universe set out for itself and independent of us, consistent and inexhaustible It is not a world constructed by us; we penetrate into it as best we can through those central openings that are our axioms and postulates.

Whence do the objects present to our intellect derive their power to raise it to higher and higher levels in the diverse degrees of the scale of truth, or adequation of mind to being? What makes the universe of number superior in its truth to the truths of experience, from which our intellect has made that universe emerge, and to which it is irreducible? There must be a cause that possesses in its own right that perfection that is truth, or adequation of mind and being, and that is at once the transcendent First Cause of the intelligibility of being in its diverse degrees, and of the acts of intellection that correspond to it. In other words, there must be a First Cause that is subsistent Truth, or the Intellection of itself by itself subsisting through itself—subsisting, I mean, in the absolute identity of mind and being, since the essence of the Being-through-itself is its intellect, and its intellect is its very essence.

Thus the noble Augustinian approach, which rises to God through eternal truths, finds its normal place in the fourth way of Thomas Aquinas.

11. *The Fifth Way: By the Governance of Things.* On this planet, where but little time is given us to pass from the womb to the tomb, men alone are endowed with intelligence. It is a fact that in this universe myriads of beings exist and act but neither know nor think. And it is a fact that the activities of all these beings follow regular courses, which are translated into the laws that our science establishes, and which give rise to recurrences of constant periodicity. All these beings evolve; they advance in time. The movement of their history is irreversible, but their evolution itself takes place in conformity with the laws of nature and moves in a definite direction, about which science brings us more and more

precise information. Whether one considers the actions that they exert upon one another or the general movement of their history, things are thus seen to be engaged in a system of regular relations and orientated in a stably defined direction.

This in itself shows that a purpose, not chance, is at work in the world. In fact, *constancies* and a *stable orientation* in the midst of the diverse is enough to prevent the reduction of everything to chance, because they require a *raison d'être*, which cannot be found in the diverse as such.

Does this mean that the universe must be regarded as a machine, in other words, as an arrangement of parts bound together by extrinsic connections (and differentiated from one another by extrinsic modifications, so that they are ultimately reducible to the purely homogeneous, as in the pure mechanism of a Descartes)? Such a hypothesis is, in my opinion, philosophically erroneous. At any rate, it is impossible to hold it without positing at the same time (and in a quite anthropomorphic perspective) a purpose at the origin of the world; for the very notion of a machine (in which everything depends upon an arrangement of material parts that does not derive from the materials themselves) supposes a plan or pattern in the mind, according to which it is made. Even if one were to admit that a machine might develop all by itself out of a simple initial state, it would still presuppose a plan or pattern in the mind to explain its origin.

If the world is not a machine, then it must be a republic of *natures*, each of which is an internal principle of activity. The fact that things are engaged in a system of regular relations and orientated in a stably defined direction signifies that they have natures that are root tendencies, identical with definite ontological structures. But every tendency is by definition a tendency to something; in other words, it is determined by the term toward which it is orientated. Now, what is this term toward which a tendency is orientated, if not something to be attained, in a word an end (which, as such, exists only as the object of the intention of an intellect)?

If this end assigned to things exists only in our mind, the tendency in question also exists only in our mind. We attribute it metaphorically to things; it does not really exist in them. If on the contrary the tendency in question really exists in things—if it is a basic tendency identical with a certain ontological structure—it is because the end that determines it exists in an intellect at work in things.

But the things that compose the world of matter are devoid of knowledge and understanding; no intention to an end can proceed from them. This intention must exist in an intellect on which things depend—and which is at once omnipresent and separate from things.

Let it be remarked in passing that the concepts that we have just employed, notably that of "nature," have their functional equivalents not only in the not yet technically elaborated notions of common sense, but in every metaphysics that—even with conceptualizations and notional perspectives entirely different from those of the Aristotelian and Thomistic metaphysics—is aware of the variety and of the mysterious ontological energy immanent in the real.

Thus it is ultimately necessary to come at last to an intellect that has the intention of the ends to which things and their natures tend, and that brings that intention into being, not only at the origin of the world, but incessantly, without itself depending, either for existence or for the activation of things and natures toward their ends, on another intellect which precedes it in being. In other words, it is necessary to come at last to a transcendent First Cause, the existing of which is its very intellection, and which directs things toward their ends—without itself being subject to the causality of any end—through the very act by which it wills its own goodness, which is its very being.

11A.—a) Should it be said that Thomas Aquinas, in his exposition of the fifth way, asserts that the intention of an end "appears from the fact that things act always or for the most part in the same way, so as to achieve that which is best, *ut consequantur id quod est optimum*"; but that it is quite impossible to verify such a result, especially in a world so full of miseries as ours, one might answer:

It is certainly quite impossible to verify such a result. But the assertion of St. Thomas signifies only that from the fact that things act always, or act for the most part, in the same way, it follows that they act as orientated toward an end. Now such an orientation, by the very fact that it assures the perseverance of things in being, tends toward the good of things in general. Consequently, the conditions proper to the particular structure of our world being given, it is the greatest good possible *in relation to these conditions* that will result from the activity of things—an entirely relative optimism to tell the truth, and one compatible with the bitterest views of Ecclesiastes on this valley of tears (an optimism moreover that does not rest on verification, but on logical inference).

b) Should one insist that according to the mathematical computation of chances, the world *could* be the effect of chance, however slight the probability, just as the *Iliad* could, however slight the probability, result from the fortuitous juxtaposition of letters thrown down at random, there is a further answer.

All arguments of this sort drawn from the calculation of probabilities are based on a double sophism or a double illusion. [1]. An effect can be due to chance only if some datum aside from chance is presupposed at the origin. To cast letters at random presupposes letters and presupposes the hand that casts them with this intention, or an instrument constructed for that purpose. The predictions made by the actuaries presuppose the innumerable causal lines on whose mutual interference the duration of a human organism depends. Statistical laws presuppose the existence of causal laws that can be unknown but according to which the things and the energies of nature operate in certain given fields—without which, indeed, the great number of fortuitous occurrences on which the certainty of statistical laws depends simply could not happen.

[2]. By the very fact that one applies the calculation of chances to a given case (for instance, what is the probability that in a series of casts of the die the die will fall on a given side? What is the probability that a given number will come forth from among

all the numbers in a lottery?), one adopts from the outset a perspective in which the *possibility* of the event in question has been admitted from the start. (I ask what the probability is that the die will fall on this side, or that a given number will issue from the lottery, only because I know to begin with that a die *can* fall on any one of its sides or that any number at all *can* come forth from among those in a lottery.) To say—and this makes sense only *on the hypothesis* in which it would be legitimate to apply the calculation of chances to the case—that, however slight be the probability, there is still one chance in the incalculable myriads of myriads of chances that the world is the effect of chance, implies that one has admitted from the outset that the world *can* be the effect of chance. To attempt to demonstrate that the world can be the effect of chance by beginning with the presupposition of this very possibility is to become the victim of a patent sophism or a gross illusion. In order to have the right to apply the calculus of probabilities to the case of the formation of the world, it would be necessary first to have established that the world can be the effect of chance. And it is the same in regard to the *Iliad*.[14]

c) Thomas Aquinas, in the fifth way, employs extrinsic finality as a medium of demonstration because it is the most apparent and most manifest kind of finality. It would do equally well to posit an *ordered multitude of "free" elements*, or of elements not bound to one another as parts of a machine, and to posit this multiplicity *in time*, in order to see that such a multiplicity could not persevere in being, as an ordered multitude, if it were not directed. In establishing that the movement of the world in time is itself ordered or tends in a certain definite direction, modern science confirms and, so to speak, strengthens the certainty of this conclusion.

Let it be noted at this point that St. Thomas might have employed as means of demonstration the *intrinsic* or *immanent* finality that characterizes living beings. A living organism tends toward an end that remains within it, and which is itself, or rather its own preservation and its own fulfillment in being, and its own perpetuation (nutrition, growth, reproduction). But since the living organism does not tend toward such an end by knowing it, willing it and taking the means of attaining it (plant, animal, or man, it lives but is entirely unaware of the ways and means of its own life), it is quite obvious that the tendency to the end, which proceeds in it from something that is consubstantial with it (what Aristotle called its "form" or its "entelechy"), must depend on an intellect outside of it in which the intention of the end exists.

Finally, St. Thomas could have used, as means of demonstration, the *primitive* or *radical* finality that is the *raison d'être* of the very causality of every efficient cause. No agent would act if it did not tend toward an end.[15] Then it is apparent that the immediate end of the action of any agent whatever (which is the reason-for-being of its activity) is itself—being good, but not Absolute Goodness—ordered to a superordinated better end. The common good of the universe is better than the immediate good or end of any whatsoever of its parts. One is therefore, in the last analysis, necessarily led to an end that is the ultimate end of, or reason for, the action of every agent (and of the common good of the universe of nature, which is itself not the Absolute Good either); such an end, not being itself ordered to any other end, is necessarily subsistent Good itself, or subsistent Goodness. One must further conclude that no agent would act, or tend toward its end, if it were not primarily tending toward the subsistent Good. It is in virtue of their movement toward God, the transcendent ultimate End, and of the love with which every being naturally loves God more than itself, that all agents whatsoever in action in the world move toward their proper end.

12. The five ways of Thomas Aquinas[16] not only constitute five typically distinct arguments; but, as the reader has no doubt remarked during the course of this exposition, they are also distributed in a certain order in which the depth of the thought and the complexity of the discussion increase. In proportion as the mind delves deeper into the world of experience in order to reach the first starting point of its thinking, it discerns in the First Being more and more meaningful aspects, and richer perspectives are disclosed to it.

These five ways, as they are put forth in the *Prima Pars* of the *Summa Theologica*, question 2, article 3, lead of themselves to the existence of a First Being, the cause of all the others. This is—at the stage of "nominal definition" (but there is no *definition* of God)—what everyone understands by the word *God*.

In the following articles, where it is established that the First Being is pure Act and that in him essence and existence are strictly identical, the proof is achieved and completed. At that moment, we are able to see what it is that makes the First Being to be truly God, what it is that properly characterizes that First Being as God, namely, his infinite transcendence, and his essential and infinite distinction from all other beings.

Although the creation and conservation of things are one and the same action in God, they are distinct where things are concerned. God *creates* things without using any intermediary—nothing created can serve as instrument for the creation of another thing (because an instrument disposes a pre-existent matter, and there is here no pre-existent matter). But God *conserves* things in being by employing as an intermediary cause the activity of agents, themselves created, which concur instrumentally to maintain one another in existence.

It follows from this that if one considers the five ways as leading to the First Cause insofar as it *conserves* things in being, the demonstration, proceeding from the axiom "One cannot go on infinitely in the series of causes," envisages a series of causes superordinated to one another that is really given as a matter of fact, although we might be more or less at a loss to put our finger on each of these diverse causes in particular. Besides, it suffices for our argument to make them up as we please.

But if the ways are considered as leading to the First Cause insofar as it *creates* things in being, the demonstration, proceeding from the axiom "One cannot go on infinitely in the series of causes" envisages a series of causes superordinated to one another that, as a matter of fact, is not really given. We may imagine these diverse causes as we please—they remain imaginary. They provide logical aid to the demonstration. We may suppose that they exist, and then it becomes clear that to rise from cause to cause endlessly is impossible. In reality, however, the First Cause to which one is thus led—the Cause that is beyond all possible series in the world of experience—is the only cause that causes in the sense of *creating* (causing things *ex nihilo*).

For all that, it is clear that this very fact, that things are created, is only known by us once we know that the First Cause exists; consequently, we cannot make use of it in order to demonstrate the existence of that First Cause. All we know from the outset is that things are caused. And it is on the fact that they are caused (not on the fact that they are created, nor on the fact that they are conserved in being) that we take our stand in order to rise to the necessary existence of the First Cause—without as yet distinguishing between causation which conserves and causation that creates, but rather by prescinding from this distinction. These remarks indicate the kind of answer required to meet the difficulty raised by Mortimer Adler in regard to the five ways,[17] a difficulty springing from his anticipating in his initial outlook the perspective that the idea of creation opens up, whereas the idea of causation is the only one and should be the only one to enter here.

NOTES

1. In the proposition "Everything that is contingent is caused," the predicate is not contained in the notion of the subject, but the subject is necessarily contained—as proper subject— in the notion of the predicate. This is what Thomists call a proposition known of itself *per se secundo modo*. See our book *Reflexions sur l'Intelligence* (Paris: Desclée de Brouwer, 4th ed., 1938), 71–72. "Consequently, it is the subject that belongs to the notion of the predicate, not as an intrinsic part of its structure but as the proper matter, or subject, in which it is received; for the notion of accident or property cannot be understood without that of subject (thus, *nasus* belongs to the notion of *simus, number* belongs to the notion of *odd* or *even*). This second sort of *a priori* 'synthesis' or construction of necessary concepts which Cajetan calls *complexio extrasubstantialis* (synthesis by what lies outside

the subject), and which Leibniz and the moderns, neglecting all that pertains to material causation, have utterly forgotten, is, by special title, a notional passage from other to other; for here, the predicate is not drawn from the notion or definition of the subject, but the real identity upon which it rests always remains as demanded by the notions themselves, one of which designates the proper subject of the other; and it thus stands in contrast to what obtains in propositions belonging to the experimental order. Such is the case, for instance, in respect to the principle of causality—to choose an example among propositions of this sort which are known immediately and without any *discursus: to be caused* does not constitute part of the definition of *contingent being*, but it is a property, a *propria passio*, whose proper subject is contingent being."

2. See *Les Degrés du Savoir*, chap. 2, 102 ff.; *The Philosophy of Nature* (New York: Philosophical Library, 1951), chap. 3, 140–144.

3. These ways are set forth in the *Summa Theologica*, I, q.2, a.3. (See text 3 in the appendix.) We propose to restate the very same arguments, divesting them, however, of all the examples borrowed from ancient physics and formulating them in language appropriate to our times.

4. In the interesting dialogue that Viscount Samuel engaged in with his friend Einstein and with the contemporary physicists (Herbert L. Samuel, president of the British Institute of Philosophy, *Essay in Physics*, 1951 [New York: Harcourt Brace, 1952]), Einstein takes the part of science, while Viscount Samuel sides with philosophy. Yet it happens that Einstein links science to a disappointing philosophy, and defends the methodological approach and the type of conceptualization proper to mathematical physics (except where Heisenberg's "principle of indeterminacy" is concerned), but in asking support from the postulates of German idealism. Viscount Samuel, on the other hand, links philosophy to an amphibious science (at once physicomathematical and Aristotelian) and defends the demands of a sane philosophical realism, but at the same time he remains throughout on the level of science and uses there, in part at least,

the methodological approach and the type of conceptualization proper to ancient physics.

In both cases the distinction between ontological knowledge and empiriological knowledge is completely missed. Viscount Samuel does not appear to have advanced beyond the conception of philosophy that prevailed at the time of Newton and the classical age of the British philosophies of nature. Were one to suppose, which is not likely, that physics would commit itself to the procedures he indicates, the hope of establishing a genuine philosophy of nature on the concepts worked out by physical theories would remain futile.

The fact is, however, that a thinker of such recognized authority as Viscount Samuel refuses to accept the notion of "state of motion," demands with Aristotle a moving cause to account for the continuation of the movement of projectiles, and undertakes, with the liberty of mind and disrespect of an iconoclast, to ruin the principle of inertia and that First Newtonian Law of motion (cf. note 5 below), which Whitehead wanted to hear chanted as the first article of the creed of science in the great halls of universities. (A. N. Whitehead, *Essays in Science and Philosophy* [London: Rider & Co., 1948], 171.)

5. Cf. the classical formula set down by Newton in his First Law of Motion: *Every body continues in a state of rest, or of uniform motion in a straight line, unless it is compelled to change that state by forces impressed upon it.*

In the dynamics of Einstein, the state of motion in which a body perseveres of itself is a state not of uniform motion but of uniformly accelerated motion. In this case, the action of a cause would be required to change the acceleration. Thus it would still be true that every change in its state of movement is due to "another."

6. St. Thomas seems to have hesitated on this question. But finally, going back over what he had written (in 1266–68) in the *Summa Theologica* (I, 7, 4), he declares in *De Aeternitate Mundi* (written about 1270–71): "And yet one has not yet demonstrated that God cannot produce infinite things in act (an infinite multitude in act)." Thus, he made room in advance for the logical

validity of the speculations of modern mathematics on infinite multitude. If the world had been created *ab aeterno,* and if human generations had succeeded one another during the infinity of a time without beginning, an infinite multitude of immortal souls would exist in act. An infinite multitude in act is not *formed* or numerable, but it does not imply contradiction. A transfinite number (which is not an *infinite number* but the symbol designating an infinite multitude supposed as given in act) is a mathematical *ens rationis,* but does not imply contradiction in its concept.

7. *Summa Theologica,* I, 46, 2.

8. Cf. "Reflections on Necessity and Contingence," *Essays in Thomism,* ed. by Robert E. Brennan, OP (New York: Sheed & Ward, 1942).

9. Bossuet.

10. When it comes to perfections that relate to the transcendental order, the phrase *per se* ("through itself") or *per suam essentiam* and the phrase *per essentiam* ("in essence," as I put it) coincide in their application, though they differ in formal meaning. To say that a thing is necessary *per se* or *per suam essentiam* is to say that the predicate "necessary" belongs to this subject (this thing) by virtue of the essence of the latter. To say that a thing is necessary *per essentiam* is to say that the subject (the thing in question) is one with the very essence of this predicate. See Cajetan, in *Sum. Theol.,* I, 6, 3.

11. Among these values we have mentioned knowledge and love—inasmuch as, through a kind of infinity proper to the soul in its spiritual functions, knowledge and love have in the soul, intentionally, the same transcendental value as being and good which are their object.

But it is possible to go further, and I think that a fully realistic metaphysics should regard knowledge and love as themselves constituting transcendentals or *passiones entis.* Below knowledge in the strict sense of the word (which implies immateriality), one can as a matter of fact call *knowledge,* in a physical sense, *action,* which, insofar as it joins the agent and the patient and is their common act, is a sort of *co-esse* between different things. The notion of knowledge thus enlarged is, hence, no longer limited to the subjects which have the privilege of knowledge properly so called; it appears as coextensive with that of Being; being and knowing (*co-naître*, as Claudel says) are convertible.

Likewise, since there is an *amor naturalis* that is but one with things and inclines them toward their end, the notion of love is not limited to subjects capable of producing acts of elicited love; it is coextensive with that of Being; to be and to love are convertible.

As to life, it is nothing but the transcendental Being itself in its highest form.

12. Of the same logical type as the principle of causality. Cf. p. 21, note 1 above.

13. A body that possesses a quality—heat, elasticity, etc.—to any degree at all obviously "participates" in the nature of this quality, but it does not participate in it as in a quality or perfection that tends by reason of itself to the absolute. It participates in it as in a quality or perfection of a generic order which, being conceivable only under the limitations proper to such or such genus of things of which it is an accident, does not admit of a pure state. It does not possess it by participation in a perfection which, inasmuch as it overflows or transcends every genus and every category of beings, demands to exist in a pure or absolute state, hence in a "first" which possesses it *per se* and in a formal-eminent manner.

14. Some letter cast by chance can form a group that appears to the mind as a word, but this group is not in reality a sign, a bearer of meaning. As soon as the function of signification is *real*, the assemblage *cannot* result by chance.

15. Cf. *A Preface of Metaphysics* (New York: Sheed & Ward, 1940), chap. 5 and 6.

16. These ways are philosophical or purely rational proofs, but they are set forth by a theologian in a theological context. For one who recognizes the proper value of theology, it is apparent that by this fact they are brought to a higher degree of rational purity and of condensation without anything being changed in

their strictly philosophical nature. They are, as it were, the flower or the quintessence of the inquiry that philosophy conducts in advancing by slower steps and in starting closer to the earth than theology does. (I think that in a complete philosophical treatise on theodicy the metaphysical demonstration would be preceded by many a digression of an order more experimental than rational.) The work of philosophy is found superelevated *in its proper order* when the theologian takes it over and rethinks it in the perspective of a superior wisdom.

17. Cf. Mortimer J. Adler, "The Demonstration of God's Existence," in the Maritain volume of *The Thomist* (New York: Sheed & Ward, 1943).

CHAPTER 3

A SIXTH WAY

13. The views which I propose here are based neither on a fact observed in the world of sense experience, nor on the principle "One cannot rise to the infinite in the series of causes," nor does the argument proceed with the royal simplicity of the ways of Thomas Aquinas. It may, indeed, appear too subtle, and for a long time I regarded it as belonging to the domain of research hypotheses. I have, however, come to think that it constitutes a genuine proof, a rationally valid way leading to a firmly established certitude.

Here again it is appropriate to distinguish two levels of approach—a *pre-philosophic* level whereon certitude bathes in an intuitive experience, and a *scientific* or *philosophical* level whereon certitude emanates from a logically elaborated demonstration and from a rationally developed metaphysical justification.

We shall first take our stand on the pre-philosophic level. Indeed, it is the intuitive process that, in this case more than ever, matters first of all, although the intuition in question is of a much more peculiar sort than the primordial intuition of existing, and supposes experience of the proper life of the intellect. By feeling the impact of this intuitive experience, the mind discovers the approach to God that this experience brings along with it. Later it is led to formulate in logically conceptualized terms that which I call here a "sixth way."

The intuition of which I speak is related to the natural spirituality of intelligence. I shall try to describe it as it is in its primitive and, so to speak, "wild" state, where it first begins to sprout.

I am busy thinking. Everything in me is concentrated on a certain truth that has caught me up in its wake. This truth carries me off. All the rest is forgotten. Suddenly I come back to myself; a reflection is awakened in me which seems to me quite incongruous, altogether unreasonable, but whose evidence takes possession of me, in my very perception of my act of thought: *how is it possible that I was born?*

The activity of the mind develops in two quite different orders. It develops on the one hand in the order of the life that Aristotle called "life proportioned to man." Here the activity of the mind, as it happens in our train of ordinary social or occupational pursuits, is made up of a succession of operations immersed in time and which are for the most part operations of sense and imagination sustained and illuminated by the intellect.

On the other hand, it develops in the order of the life that Aristotle called "life proportioned to the intellect." Here the activity of the mind, entirely withdrawn in thought, is centered above the sense and imagination, and is concerned with intelligible objects alone. It is when a man is thus engaged in an act of purely intellectual thought (to the extent that this is possible for a rational animal) that it happens that the intuition in question takes place: how is it possible that that which is thus in the process of thinking, in the act of intelligence, which is immersed in the fire of knowledge and of intellectual grasp of what is, should once have been a pure nothing, once did not exist? Where I am now in the act of intellection and of consciousness of my thought, was there once *nothing?* That is impossible; it is not possible that at a certain moment what is now thinking was not at all, was a pure nothing. How could this have been born to existence?

I am not here faced with a logical contradiction. I am facing a *lived* contradiction, an incompatibility (known *in actu exercito*). It is as if I were in a room and, without my having left for an instant, someone were to say to me that I just came in—I know that what he says is impossible.

Thus, I who am now in the act of thinking have always existed. This view imposes itself on me and does not seem strange to me unless I draw myself back from it in order to consider it from without. And perhaps I express it in a deficient way; we shall see about that later. For the moment, I speak as I can, and I cannot speak otherwise.

Yet I know quite well that I was born. True, I know it by hearsay, but I do know it with an absolute certainty, and besides, I remember my childhood. The certitude of having been born, common to all men, represses in us the blossoming forth—when the natural spirituality of intelligence is activated in us—of another certitude, that of the impossibility that our existence as thinking minds ever began or followed upon the nothingness of itself, and it prevents that other certitude from reaching our consciousness.

So here I am, in the grasp of two contrary certitudes. There is only one solution: I, who am thinking, have always existed, but not in myself or within the limits of my own personality—and not by an impersonal existence or life either (for without personality there is no thought, and there must have been thought there, since it is now in me); therefore I have always existed by a suprapersonal existence or life. Where then? It must have been in a Being of transcendent personality, in whom all that there is of perfection in my thought and in all thought existed in a supereminent manner, and who was, in his own infinite Self, before I was, and is, now while I am, more I than I myself, who is eternal, and from whom I, the self which is thinking now, proceeded one day into temporal existence. I had (but without being able to say "I") an eternal existence in God before receiving a temporal existence in my own nature and my own personality.

14. What shall we say now if we transport ourselves onto the level of rational demonstration? Is it possible to justify philosophically the intuitive experience that we have just tried to describe?

What is important to consider first is that the intellect is above time, *intellectus supra tempus*: because the intellect is spiritual, and time, the perseverance of movement in being, or the continuity of perpetually vanishing existence proper to movement, is the proper duration of matter.

47

The operations of the human intellect are in time, and, indeed, subject to time, but in an extrinsic manner and only by reason of the materiality of the senses and the imagination to whose exercise they are bound. In themselves they are not subject to the flux of impermanence. They emerge above time. They exist in a duration that is a deficient imitation of eternity, a succession of fragments of eternity, for it is the perseverance in being of spiritual acts of intellection or of contemplative gaze. Thus this duration is composed of instants superior to time, each of which may correspond to a lapse of time more or less long, but is in itself without flow or movement or succession—a flash of permanent or nonsuccessive existence. Such is the proper duration of thought. Thought as such is not in time. The distinction between the *spiritual* and the *temporal* appears here in its primary sense. That which is spiritual is not subject to time. The proper place of the spiritual is above temporal existence.

We find a noteworthy indication of this in the fact that spiritual events are "metahistorical" events. Insofar as they are occurrences, they take place in history, but their content belongs in a region superior to history. This is why it is normal for history not to mention them. The word *event* itself is therefore ambiguous. "What happens," in the case of spiritual events, comes on the scene for an instant in temporal existence, but comes forever in the existence of souls and of thought.

But actions or operations emanate from a subject or from a person—*actiones sunt suppositorum*. And no operation is more personal than thought. Thought is exercised by a certain subject, a certain *self*, made of flesh and spirit.

This self exists in time and was born in time. But inasmuch as it exercises the spiritual operation of thought, inasmuch as it is the center of spiritual activity and capable of living or existing by the immaterial superexistence of the act of intellection, it is also superior to time, as is thought itself. It escapes the grasp of time.

This self began in time. But nothing begins absolutely. Everything that begins existed before itself in a certain way, to wit, in its causes. Insofar as it is material, the thinking self existed before itself in time, namely, in the ancestral cells, the physicochemical materials and energies utilized by life all along the line from which the self has sprung. Whatever of it existed before it pre-existed in time.

But as spiritual, as exercising the spiritual operations of thought, as thinking, it could not have existed before itself in time, because mind can come only from a mind, thought can come only from a thought, and therefore from an existence superior to time.

Moreover, since thought is essentially personal, when it arises in time as the operation of such and such a subject born one day into temporal existence, it cannot come from an existence superior to time unless the self that exercises it now pre-existed in a certain way beyond time.

The self is born in time. But insofar as it is thinking, it is not born of time. Its birth is supratemporal. It existed before itself in a first existence distinct from every temporal existence. It did not exist there in its proper nature (since it began to exist in its proper nature by being born in time), but everything that there is in it of being and of thought and of personality existed there better than in itself.

This, however, would not be possible unless everything that exists in temporal existence were a participation of the first existence in question. The latter then must contain all things in itself in an eminent mode and be itself—in an absolutely transcendent way—being, thought and personality. This implies that that first existence is the infinite plenitude of being, separate by essence from all the diversity of existents. This means that it is not the act of existing of a thing which *has* existence, but the very act of existing itself, subsisting through itself. Thus, we are necessarily led to the principle that no concept can circumscribe—Being in pure act, from which comes every being; Thought in pure act from which comes every thought; Self in pure act from which comes every self.

It is thus that the "sixth way" leads us to the existence of God. But it would remain incompletely elucidated if, after recognizing the existence of God, we should not ask ourselves how things exist in him before being caused by him in their own *esse*.[1]

Things pre-exist in God not in their proper natures but according as they are known to God, and, therefore, by that which renders them present to the divine intellect, that is to say by the divine essence itself, of which they are participations or likenesses, and which is itself the proper object of the divine intellect. In God they are the divine essence as revealing its participability. They live there, but without existing in themselves, by a life infinitely more perfect than the existence that they have in their proper natures. They live, in God who knows them, by the very life of God. They exist in the divine thought by the very existence of God that is his act of intellection.

This is true of thinking subjects, of *selves* endowed with intelligence, as it is of all other creatures. Before existing in themselves, they exist eternally in God by the very existence of God, as participations or likenesses of the divine essence eternally known in that Essence. Therefore I can say that I, who am now in the act of thinking, always existed—I always existed in God. Care must be taken, however, to understand this proposition correctly. It does not mean that in God the human self has always exercised the act of thinking, or that in God it collaborates eternally in the act of divine thought. That makes no sense. In God, the unique Self who thinks is the divine Self. The statement signifies rather that the creature which is now I, and which thinks, existed before itself eternally in God—not as exercising in him the act of thinking, but as thought by him. It bathed there in the light of God; it lived there by a suprapersonal (suprapersonal in relation to every created personality) and divinely personal life, by that life which is the eternal act of intellection of the divine Self itself, thinking itself.

Thinking subjects, *selves* capable of acting beyond time, which thus pre-exist in God, as do all those other participations of the Divine Essence which are created things—infinitely deficient in relation to their principle—are the most elevated of all things in the whole order of nature, because they are either purely spiritual creatures or creatures composed of matter and spirit, which, once they exist in their proper nature, resemble the divine Self in that they think and can be called, because of this, "images of God."

A Sixth Way

The reflections we have proposed in this chapter, as well as the intuitive experience which they presuppose, are entirely independent of any contact with Indian thought. It seems to us nevertheless that they can help to clarify in some way the meaning and the origin of the Hindu notion of the Self (*Atman*), and throw into relief at once the metaphysical truths to which this notion is related and the confusion which it has not succeeded in avoiding between the divine Self and the human self.

On the other hand, the importance accorded to the expression *not-born* in many Hindu texts[2] seems to us to suggest a quite remarkable affinity with the intuition of which we have treated here, and to indicate that an intuition of the same type plays a characteristic role in the philosophic thought and the natural mysticism of India.

NOTES

1. Cf. *Summa Theologica*, I, 18, 4, corp. et ad 3.

2. Cf. Louis Gardet, *Expériences mystiques en terres nonchrétiennes* (Paris: Alsatia, 1953), 38–39. Let us take up in particular this passage of the *Katha Upanishad*: "The inspired, the Atman, is not born nor dies. It does not come from anywhere, and it does not become anyone. Not-born, permanent, constant, primordial, it is not destroyed when the body is destroyed." And this passage of the *Yoga-sutra*: "When thought is not dissolved and ceases dispersing itself, neither unstable, nor endowed with images, it becomes then the Brahman. Free, calm, having an inexpressible beatitude, a supreme happiness, not-born with an object of knowledge itself not-born, omniscient, behold how one defines it."

See also Olivier Lacombe, "Sur le Yoga Indien (Report of Ramana Maharshi)," *Etudes Carmélitaines* (October 1937): 174–175; *La Doctrine Morale et Métaphysique de Râmânuja* (Paris: Adrien-Maisonneuve, 1938), 63–68.

CHAPTER 4

THE WAYS OF THE
PRACTICAL INTELLECT

15. *Poetic Experience and Creation in Beauty.* The diverse ways
of which we have so far spoken are ways of the speculative intellect. The practical intellect also has its ways of approach towards
God—which are not demonstrations at all but belong to an existential and pre-philosophic order. I shall give here some brief
indications concerning them.

There is first, in the line of artistic creation, what one might
call the analogy of the approach to God in poetic experience, or
the poetic knowledge of the mirrors of God.

The artist is held in the grip of a twofold absolute, which is not
the Absolute, but which draws the soul toward it. The demands of
that beauty which must pass into his work, and the demands of that
poetry which incites him to create, claim him so entirely that, in a
certain way, they cut him off from the rest of men.

Beauty is a transcendental, a perfection in things that transcends things and attests their kinship with the infinite, because
it makes them fit, to give joy to the spirit. It is a reflection in
things of the Spirit from which they proceed, and it is a divine
name: God is subsistent Beauty, and "the being of all things
derives from the divine beauty."[1] Knowing this, we realize that it
is impossible that the artist, devoted as he is to created beauty
which is a mirror of God, should not tend at the same time—but
by a more profound and more secret urge than all that he can
know of himself—toward the principle of beauty.

A celebrated passage of Baudelaire, inspired by Edgar Allan
Poe, reveals in this connection its full import, the import of an

unimpeachable testimony: "...it is this immortal instinct for the beautiful which makes us consider the earth and its various spectacles as a sketch of, as a *correspondence* with, heaven. The insatiable thirst for all that is beyond, and which life reveals, is the most living proof of our immortality. It is at once through poetry and *across* poetry, through and *across* music, that the soul glimpses the splendors situated beyond the grave; and when an exquisite poem brings tears to the eyes, these tears are not proof of an excess of joy, they are rather the testimony of an irritated melancholy, a demand of the nerves, of a nature exiled in the imperfect and desiring to take possession immediately, even on this earth, of a revealed paradise."[2]

Knowledge, not rational and conceptual, but affective and nostalgic, the knowledge through connaturality which the artist has of beauty in his creative experience, is *in itself* (I do not say for him or for his own consciousness) an advance toward God, a spiritual inclination in the direction of God, an obscure and ill-assured beginning of the knowledge of God—vulnerable, indeed, on all sides because it is not disengaged in the light of intelligence and because it remains without rational support.

Poetry is the prime and pure actuation of the free creativity of the spirit. Awakened in the unconscious of the spirit, at the root of all the powers of the soul, it reveals to the poet, in the obscure knowledge that is born of an intuitive emotion, both his own subjectivity and the secret meanings of things. "The poet completes the work of creation, he cooperates in divine balancings, he moves mysteries about."[3] Poetic experience is a brooding repose which "acts as a bath of refreshment, rejuvenation, and purification of the mind," and which, born of a contact with reality that is in itself ineffable, seeks liberation in song.

> It is a concentration of all the energies of the soul, but a pacific, tranquil concentration, which involves no tension. The soul enters into its repose, in this place of refreshment and of peace superior to any feeling. It dies 'the death of the Angels,' but only to revive in exaltation and enthusiasm, in that state which is

wrongly called inspiration—wrongly, for inspiration was nothing else indeed than this very repose, in which it escaped from sight. Now the mind, invigorated and vivified, enters into a happy activity, so easy that everything seems to be given it at once and, as it were, from the outside. In reality, everything was there, kept in the shade, hidden in the spirit and in the blood; all that which will be manifested in operation was already there, but we knew it not. We knew neither how to discover nor how to use it, before having gained new forces in those tranquil depths.[4]

Poetic experience differs in nature from mystical experience. It is concerned with the created world and with the innumerable enigmatic relations of beings with one another, while mystical experience is concerned with the principle of beings in its unity superior to the world. The obscure knowledge through connaturality proper to poetic experience proceeds from an emotion which shakes the recesses of subjectivity, while the more obscure but more decisive and more stable knowledge through connaturality proper to mystical experience proceeds—either, in the natural mystical experience, from a purely intellectual concentration which produces a void in which the Self is ineffably touched or, in the supernatural mystical experience, from charity, which connaturalizes the soul to God and transcends every emotion. Poetic experience is from the beginning orientated toward expression and terminates in an uttered word; mystical experience tends toward silence and terminates in an immanent fruition of the absolute.

Thus it appears that poetic experience, in its approach to created things, is an unknowing correspondence to the mystical approach to God, a lived analogy of that knowledge (not rational and conceptual, but by union of love) which the contemplative has of God. It is in a kind of connivance with this experience that differs from it essentially; it can be touched by and interlaced with it. Of itself, it disposes the soul to aspire to it.

Furthermore, because it detects the spiritual in things and

perceives in them a something beyond them, because it is a knowledge of the mirrors of God either in the being of things or, by privation, in the hollow of their nothingness, it is an advance toward God and a spiritual inclination in the direction of God, an obscure and vulnerable beginning, not of mystical experience, but of the natural knowledge of God.

But the poet knows nothing of this, nor of the bonds which in actual existence attach poetry and beauty necessarily to God; or if he does, he knows it only in so confused a way that he can either reject, insofar as his own human choices are concerned, the *élan* which traverses his experience, or divert its trend and stop at the mirror by turning aside from the too real Immensity which it enigmatically reflects. Thus, many poets are convinced that all poetry is religious by essence, though they hardly believe in God[5] or confuse him with nature.

Others, choosing atheism, commit themselves and commit poetry to the spiritual experience of the void or the search for magical powers. The call which poetic experience normally creates in the soul toward the abyss of light of uncreated Being gives way to another call—the call toward the abyss of the interior desert visited only by vultures of illusion and phantoms of miracles.

Then poetry inevitably suffers some invisible wound, but one which can stimulate it. A poet can reject God and be a great poet.

He cannot, however, free himself from every metaphysical anguish or passion. For the nostalgia for God whom he has rejected remains immanent in the poetic experience itself, whether he wills it or not. And so he is divided in his being. True, the atheism of a poet can never be completely relied upon; surprises are always possible. The same Lautréamont who declares, "I did not merit this infamous torment, thou hideous spy of my causality! If I exist I am not another....My subjectivity and the Creator, that is too much for a brain,"[6] will soon affirm: "If one recalls the truth whence all the others flow, the absolute goodness of God and his absolute ignorance of evil, the sophisms will collapse of themselves...We have not the right to question the Creator on anything whatever."[7]

Let us acknowledge it: to confuse essences is easy for poets; it is almost normal for them (that is what Plato did not forgive them). "But if the Poet confounds everything, would it not be because in him the formative powers of the world and of the word and the divine attraction toward pacification and illumination of the spirit, toward mystical knowledge and union, are together at work? We must believe, since the poets tell us that they have discovered in their nocturnal navigations or divagations a Kingdom greater than the world, that an angel is pleased sometimes to tip their bark, so that they take a little of 'that water' of which the Gospel speaks, and do not get away without some inquietude, and some great and mysterious desire."[8]

16. *The choice of the good in the first act of freedom.* The practical intellect does not deal exclusively with artistic creation. It also, and first of all, has to do with the moral life of man. There exists in this order another approach to God, enveloped in moral experience, which one might call the moral knowledge of God.

It is not possible rationally to justify fundamental moral notions such as the notion of unconditional moral obligation, or inalienable right, or the intrinsic dignity of the human person, without rising to the uncreated Reason from which man and the world proceed and which is the subsistent Good itself. Philosophical reflection on moral life and experience has thus its own proofs of the existence of God.

But it is not of this philosophical approach that I should like to speak here. I should like to speak of a quite particular knowledge of God that is implied in the moral experience itself or in the very exercise of moral life, more precisely in the first act of choice accomplished by the will, when this act is right. I may be permitted here to draw upon the more developed study which I devoted to "the immanent dialectic of the first act of *freedom.*"[9]

When a human being is awakened to moral life, his first act is to "deliberate about himself." It is a matter of choosing his way. Psychologists speak of the "Oedipus complex"; why should moralists not speak of "Heracles' choice"? The occasion can be futile in itself; it is the motivation that counts. A child one day refrains from telling a lie; he restrains himself from it on that day, not because he risks being punished if the lie is discovered or because this was forbidden him, but simply because *it is bad.* It would not be good to do that. At this moment, the moral good with all its mysterious demands, and in the presence of which he is himself and all alone, is confusedly revealed to him in a flash of understanding. And in choosing the good, in deciding to act in such a way because it is good, he has in truth, in a manner proportioned to the capacity of his age, "deliberated about himself" and chosen his way.[10]

And now, "What does such an act imply? What is the immanent dialectic, the secret dynamism of the primal act of freedom? Let us unfold and make explicit, in terms of speculative knowledge and philosophical discourse, what is contained in the indivisible vitality, both volitional and intellectual, of this act.

"The soul, in this first moral choice, turns away from an evil action because it is evil. Thus, the intellect is aware of the distinction between good and evil, and knows that the good ought to be done because it is good. We are confronted, here, with a formal motive that transcends the whole order of empirical convenience and desire. This is the primary implication of the first act of freedom when it is good.

"But, because the value with which the moral object and the moral act are permeated surpasses anything given in empirical existence and concerns that which *ought to be,* the notion of a good action to be done for the sake of the good necessarily implies that there is an ideal and indefectible order of proper consonance between our activity and our essence, a *law* of human acts transcending all facts. This is the second implication of the first act of human freedom when it is good.

"Let us reflect upon this law. It transcends the whole empirical order; the act that I bring into existence must conform to it, if it is to be a good act; and the first precept of this law demands of me that my act be good. Such a law carries in the world of actual existence the requirements of an order that depends on a reality that is superior to everything and is Goodness itself—good by virtue of its very being, not by virtue of conformity with anything distinct from itself. Such a law manifests the existence of a Separate Good transcending all empirical existence and subsisting *per se*, and subsists primarily in this Separate Good. But how could I, in an act of total commitment, strive to achieve conformity with this transcendent law unless, by the same token and on a still more profound level, I strive toward this Separate Good and direct my life toward it because it is both *the* Good and *my* Good? The initial act which determines the direction of life and which—when it is good—chooses the good for the sake of the good, proceeds from a natural *élan* which is also, undividedly, an *élan* by which this very same act tends all at once, beyond its immediate object, toward God as the Separate Good in which the human person in the process of acting, whether he is aware of it or not, places his happiness and his end. Here we have an ordainment that is actual and formal, not virtual—but in merely lived act (*in actu exercito*), not in signified act—to God as ultimate end of human life. This is the third implication of the act of which I am speaking.

"These implications are not disclosed to the intellect of the child. They are contained in the act by which, at the term of his first deliberation about himself, he brings himself to do a good act for the sake of the moral good, of the *bonum honestum* of which he has an explicit idea, no matter how confused."[11]

It is not at all necessary that in thus performing his first human act he think explicitly of God and of his ultimate end. "He thinks of what is good and of what is evil. But by the same token he knows God, without being aware of it, he knows God because, by virtue of the internal dynamism of his choice of the good for the sake of the good, he wills and loves the Separate Good as ultimate end of his existence. Thus, his intellect has of God a vital and nonconceptual knowledge which is involved both in the practical notion (confusedly and intuitively grasped, but with its full intentional energy) of the moral good as formal motive of his first act of freedom, and in the movement of his will toward this good and, all at once, toward the Good. The intellect may already have the idea of God and it may not yet have it. The nonconceptual knowledge that I am describing takes place independently of any use possibly made or not made of the idea of God, and independently of the actualization of any explicit and conscious knowledge of man's true last End.

"In other words, the will, hiddenly, secretly, obscurely moving (when no extrinsic factor stops or deviates the process) down to the term of the immanent dialectic of the first act of freedom, goes *beyond* the immediate object of conscious and explicit knowledge (the moral good as such), and it carries with itself, down to that *beyond*, the intellect, which at this point no longer enjoys the use of its regular instruments, and, as a result, is only actualized below the threshold of reflective consciousness, in a night without concept and without utterable knowledge. The conformity of the intellect with this transcendent object, the Separate Good (attainable only by means of analogy) is then effected by the will, the rectitude of which is, in the practical order, the measure of the truth of the intellect. God is thus naturally known, without any conscious judgment, in and by the impulse of the will striving toward the Separate Good, whose existence is implicitly involved in the practical value acknowledged to the moral good. No speculative knowledge of God is achieved. This is a purely practical cognition of God, produced in and by the movement of the appetite toward the moral good precisely considered as good. The metaphysical content with which it is pregnant is not grasped as a metaphysical content; it is not released."[12]

The philosophical and theological problems that arise from these considerations have been discussed in the study from which these pages are extracted. Here we wish only to recall the fact that a radically practical, nonconceptual and nonconscious knowledge of the existence of God is present in act in the depth of the soul by virtue of the first choice of its freedom, when this choice is right. (To simplify things I considered this first choice at the moment of the awakening of the child to moral life. It is clear that such a basic choice can take place at any moment of life.) Even if his conscious reason is in complete ignorance of God, a man can thus know God, in an unconscious but real—practical, existential and volitional—way by virtue of a first free act having for its object *bonum honestum*, the ethical good.

We are not here, as in the case of the experience of the artist and of the poet, in the presence of a simple, fragile, and vulnerable beginning of the knowledge of God. We are confronted with an actual and formal knowledge, but one that takes place in the unconscious of the spirit, and is not brought to light except by the consideration of the philosopher analyzing it in the experience of others.

It follows from this that, given all the cleavages and the discords, schisms, divisions and contradictions, unknown by the subject himself, which can be produced between the conscious and the unconscious, it is possible that a man in whom the knowledge of which we speak exists in an unconscious state, may not only be ignorant of God in his conscious reason but may even take sides in his conscious reason against the existence of God (because of some conceptual mistake and error of reasoning) and profess atheism. He believes that he is an atheist. He cannot be one in reality if he has chosen, and as long as he has chosen, the way of the good for the sake of the good, in his basic moral choice. He is a pseudo-atheist. What he denies in his conscious reason is an *ens rationis*, whose constituent notes appear to him as incompatible with real existence or as bound to conditions which revolt him in nature or in humanity, a fiction of the imagination which he calls God but which is not God; he does not deny in reality the God who is the authentic object of reason and in whom he believes in the bottom of his heart without knowing it.

If, on the contrary, it is a question of a true atheist, the atheism which he professes consciously cannot coexist with that unconscious knowledge of God which is linked to the choice of the good for the sake of the good, because the true atheist denies not something which is not God and which he mistakes for God, but God himself, and by that very denial breaks the movement by which the will, in moving to the good for the sake of the good, passes beyond its intended object to the Separate Good, carrying the intellect along with it. Moreover, "positive and absolute" atheism itself has its origin in a *sui generis* moral experience whose characteristic is the rejection of all transcendence, a rejection decided upon in the first choice itself by which moral life takes form.[13] Thence the very idea of the moral good (*bonum honestum*) is intrinsically vitiated or disorganized, stamped with an inner contradiction, for it becomes the idea of the *bonum honestum taken as excluding God*. An absolute atheist can order his life to the good for the sake of the good, but it is to a corpse or an idol of the ethical good that he thus orders his life—to the good inasmuch as it excludes the Good. "He has killed the moral good by shattering and destroying the relationship with the Separate Good which it essentially implies. Moral good, duty, virtue inevitably become demands of his own perfection viewed as an absolute center, or a desolate rite of his own grandeur—or a total submission of himself to the sweet will of deified Becoming; and thus moral good, duty, virtue lose their true nature."[14]

But let us return to the man we have described as a pseudo-atheist. While denying a God which is not God, this man really believes in God. The fact remains that he is divided against himself, because certain obstacles to belief in God, which have arisen in him at the level of conscious thought and conceptual elaboration, form a barrier that prevents the existential knowledge which exists in the hidden, active workings of the unconscious (of both his intellect and will) from passing, along with their rational repercussions, into the sphere of consciousness. Such a situation is of itself abnormal.

Normally the unconscious and existential knowledge of God, linked to the first act of freedom when it is right, tends to pass into consciousness and it makes its way there. It creates in the soul dispositions and inclinations that assist reason in its conscious exercise to discover the truth that corresponds to them. *Those who do what is true come to the light* (John 3:21). In normal circumstances the man who has chosen the ethical good (*bonum honestum*) is found instinctively and unconsciously disposed to perceive, when the natural and spontaneous play of his reason is exercised on the spectacle of visible things, the existence of that invisible Good, of that Separate Good which he already knew without being aware of it by virtue of the choice of the good which he effected when he deliberated about himself in his first act of freedom. When, on the level of conscious thought—and thanks to the natural approach due to the primordial intuition of existence of which we treated at the beginning of this book; thanks also to the ways of philosophic reason—he perceives in the full light of intellectual evidence the necessity of the existence of the First Cause, he does not simply know God; he knows and *recognizes* him.

17. *The testimony of the friends of God.* It is fitting, finally, to mention, indirect as it may be, a way of approaching God, the value of which is only auxiliary, and which can be related to the order of moral experience. This way is based on testimony and example.

Our ordinary moral life is, indeed, precarious. Many elements are mingled in its structure. Some of them come from outside ourselves: from the manners and customs of the social group projected within us, and from the opinions of the world we live in. Some of them arise from the subterranean depths of our own unconscious—masked interventions which we but dimly discern. So loose in structure, so menaced by our own weakness, so complex and obscure is our everyday moral life that we naturally turn for guidance to those who can show us the way. They have found what we so feebly seek. So to them we turn—those men whom Bergson called the "heroes" of the spiritual life and whose "appeal" he saw traversing mankind.

The quest of the superhuman is natural to man; we find it in every climate of philosophic or religious nostalgia of our species. Without speaking of mirages, illusions, or forgeries that are met in such regions, an authentic quest can get involved in impasses or in byways. But that quest may also lead to the fullness of a love superior to nature that expresses itself in a wisdom ever open and a perfect freedom. It was by such signs that Bergson recognized a supreme accomplishment of human life among Christian mystics, who, he thought, alone had crossed the ultimate barriers.[15]

Consequently, according to Bergson, the philosopher may question them and find in their testimony a confirmation, or rather a "reinforcement,"[16] of that which he has himself, by means proper to a philosopher, caught sight of in the prolongation of another "line of facts." And what is the essential indication that he will receive from the mystics, "when he compresses...mystical intuition in order to express it in terms of intelligence?"[17] "God is love, and the object of love: herein lies the whole contribution of mysticism. About this twofold love, the mystic will never have done talking. His description is interminable, because what he wants to describe is ineffable. But what he does state clearly is that divine love is not a thing of God: it is God himself."[18] "As a matter of fact," Bergson added, "the mystics unanimously bear witness that God needs us, just as we need God. Why should he need us, unless it be to love us? And it is to this very conclusion that the philosopher who holds to the mystical experience must come. Creation will appear to him as God undertaking to create creators, that he may have, besides himself, beings worthy of his love."[19]

The movement of thought lived by Bergson is significant: the better we know the sanctity of the saints, and the moral life of those who have ventured to give all in order to enter into what they themselves describe as the divine union and the experience of the things of God, the more we feel that the truth alone can give such fruits, and that the certitude which sustains everything in these men cannot lie.

An act of true goodness, the least act of true goodness, is indeed the best proof of the existence of God. But our intellect is too busy cataloguing notions to see it. Therefore, we believe it on the testimony of those in whom true goodness shines in a way that astonishes us.

This is not a proof of the existence of God. It is an argument based only on testimony. Besides, I do not think—and neither did Bergson—that it is capable of winning the assent of the mind except when in other ways the mind—supposing some obstacle hinders it from feeling the full force with which the being of things manifests the existence of their Cause—is at least solicited by beginnings of proof, signs and tokens whose rational value imposes itself upon the mind. Neither do I think that this argument commands rational or purely natural assent unless there be also mingled with it a belief of another order, based on the invisible testimony, in the depths of the soul, of the God of whom we hear his friends speak.

But in the end, considering it only in the order and on the level of reason, this argument has its proper value and validity; and it is possible that in fact, in concrete existence, this auxiliary way plays, for many, a more important role than pure logicians think. I wanted in any case to mention it here, for the reasons I have just given, and in memory of the great philosopher whom it helped to discover God.

NOTES

1. St. Thomas Aquinas, *Comm. in De Divinis Nominibus*, chap. 4, lect. 5.

2. Baudelaire, "Théophile Gautier," in *L'Art Romantique*.

3. "Answer to Jean Cocteau," *Art and Faith* (New York: Philosophical Library, 1948), 90.

4. Raïssa Maritain, "Sens et Non-Sens en Poésie." In *Situation de la Poésie* 2nd ed. (Paris: Desclée, 1948), 48–49.

5. "Robert Desnos does not believe in God, nevertheless he writes: 'Nobody has a more religious mind than I...' (*Revue Européene*, mars 1924)." Raïssa Maritain, *Situation de la Poésie*, 37.

6. "Chants de Maldoror," in *Oeuvres Complètes* (Paris: G.L.M., 1938).

7. *Préface à des Poèmes Futurs* (ibid.).

8. Raïssa Maritain, "Magie, Poésie et Mystique." In *Situation de la Poésie*, 72.

9. *The Range of Reason*, chap. 6.

10. He has chosen his way and decided about the meaning of his life, inasmuch as an act of the human will, posited in time, enlists the future: that is to say, in a fragile fashion. He is not confirmed forever in such a decision; he will be able, all during his existence, to change the decision which bears on the meaning of his life, but it will only be done by an act of freedom and of deliberation about himself just as profound as that first decision.

11. *The Range of Reason*, 68–69. The *bonum honestum* is the "good as right" (contradistinguished from the "good as useful" and the "good as pleasurable"), in other words that good which is possessed of inherent moral worth and causes conscience to be obliged. More simply—and if we are neither Utilitarians nor Epicureans—we may designate the *bonum honestum* by the expression the *moral* or *ethical* good.

12. *The Range of Reason*, 70. This analysis is related solely to the natural order considered apart, abstraction being made from the interventions of another order that have a place in concrete existence. See ibid., 75–81.

13. Cf. our essay on "The Meaning of Contemporary Atheism," *The Range of Reason*, chap. 8.

14. *The Range of Reason*, 85.

15. Cf. Henri Bergson, *The Two Sources of Morality and Religion* (New York: Henry Holt, 1935), 215–216 ff.

16. *Les Deux Sources*, 266 (my translation).

17. *The Two Sources*, 241.

18. Ibid., 240.

19. Ibid., 243.

CHAPTER 5

THE DESIRE TO SEE GOD

18. It is as First Cause of things that all the proofs of the existence of God make us know God. Whether they be philosophical or pre-philosophical, the approaches to God of which our nature is capable lead us to God, known in and through his effects or in the mirror of the things which proceed from him.

But how could the intellect, knowing God in his effects, fail to aspire to know him in himself? It is natural and normal that, knowing a reality—and the most important of all—from without and by means of signs, we should desire to know it in itself and to grasp it without any intermediary. Such a desire follows from the very nature of that quest of being which essentially characterizes the intellect. There is in the human intellect a natural desire to see in his essence that very God whom it knows through the things which he has created.

But this desire to know the *First Cause through its essence* is a desire that does not know what it asks, like the sons of Zebedee when they asked to sit on the right and on the left of the Son of Man. *You do not know what you are asking*, Jesus replied to them. For to know the First Cause in its essence, or without the intermediary of any other thing, is to know the First Cause otherwise than as First Cause; it is to know it by ceasing to attain it by the very means by which we attain it, by ceasing to exercise the very act which bears us up to it. The natural desire to know the First Cause in its essence envelops within itself the indication of the impossibility in which nature is placed to satisfy it.

To know God in his essence is evidently something which transcends the powers of every created or creatable nature, for it is to possess God intuitively, in a vision in which there is no mediation of any idea, but in which the divine essence itself replaces every idea born in our mind, so that it immediately forms and determines our intellect. This is to know God divinely, as he himself knows himself and as he knows us, in his own uncreated light.

Nothing is more human than for man to desire naturally things impossible to his nature. It is, indeed, the property of a nature which is not closed up in matter like the nature of physical things, but which is intellectual or infinitized by the spirit. It is the property of a *metaphysical* nature. Such desires reach for the infinite, because the intellect thirsts for being and being is infinite. They are natural, but one may also call them transnatural. It is thus that we desire to see God; it is thus that we desire to be free without being able to sin; it is thus that we desire beatitude.[1]

To say that our intellect naturally desires to see God is to say that it naturally desires a knowledge of which nature itself is incapable. This desire is transnatural, it moves toward an end that is beyond the end for which the nature of man is constituted. According as it reaches thus for an end which transcends every end proportioned to nature, the desire to see God is an "inefficacious" desire—a desire which it is not in the power of nature to satisfy, and it is a "conditional" desire—a desire whose satisfaction is not due to nature.

Yet, according as it emanates from nature, it is a natural and necessary desire. It is not a simple velleity, a superadded desire, a desire of supererogation. It is born in the very depths of the thirst of our intellect for being; it is a nostalgia so profoundly human that all the wisdom and all the folly of man's behavior has in it its most secret reason.

And because this desire that asks for what is impossible to nature is a desire of nature in its profoundest depths, St. Thomas Aquinas asserts that it cannot issue in an absolute impossibility.[2] It is in no wise necessary that it *be* satisfied, since it asks for what is impossible for nature. But it is necessary that by some means (which is not nature) it *be able* to be satisfied, since it necessarily emanates from nature. In other words it is necessary that an order superior to nature be possible in which man is capable of that of which nature is incapable but which it necessarily desires. It is necessary that there be in man an "obediential potency" which, answering to the divine omnipotence, renders him apt to receive a life that surpasses infinitely the capacities of his nature. It is necessary that we be able to know God in his essence through a gift that transcends all the possibilities of our natural forces. It is necessary that this knowledge, impossible to nature alone, to which nature inevitably aspires, be possible through a gratuitous gift.[3]

Shall we go beyond philosophy in order to get our answer?[4] Through the night of faith it is given us to attain in his inner life—on the testimony of his word—the very God who will be intuitively grasped when faith gives way to vision. And in the intellect elevated to the life of faith, the natural desire to see God supernaturally becomes a desire which knows what it asks for—a knowledge of God through his essence, *such as he gives himself, in his own uncreated light*—and which from now on has *in germ* the wherewithal to attain what it asks for.

Thus the natural desire to see that First Cause whose existence is shown to us through the natural approaches to God is, in human reason, the mark of the possibility—through a gift which transcends the whole order of nature, and in which God communicates what belongs only to himself—of a knowledge of God superior to reason, which is not due to reason, but to which reason aspires.

NOTES

1. On the transnatural desire for beatitude, or of absolutely and definitively saturating happiness, as distinct from the strictly natural desire for happiness or felicity in general, see our *Neuf Leçons sur les Notions Premières de la Philosophie Morale* (Paris: Téqui, 1950), 97–98.

2. Cf. *Summa Theologica*, I, 12, 1; and our work *Les Degrés du Savoir*, 562, n1.

3. Thus the argumentation of St. Thomas in the question 12, a.l, of the *Prima Pars*, establishes rationally the *possibility*, I

do not say of *the supernatural order* such as the faith presents it to us and as it implies the specifically Christian notion of grace, but of *an order superior to nature*, the notion of which remains still indeterminate, except in this, that through the divine generosity man can therein be rendered capable of knowing God in his essence.

    4. Cf. *Neuf Leçons sur les Notions Premières de la Philosophie Morale*, 102–108.

APPENDIX

Texts

1
Chāndogya Upanishad 6. 2. 2[1]

In the beginning, my dear, this was Being alone, one only without a second. Some people say 'in the beginning this was non-being alone, one only; without a second. From that non-being, being was produced.'

But how, indeed, my dear, could it be thus? said he, how could being be produced from non-being? On the contrary, my dear, in the beginning this was being alone, one only, without a second.

2
Chāndogya Upanishad 6. 8. 6

All these creatures, my dear, have their root in Being. They have Being as their abode, Being as their support.

3
St. Thomas, *Summa Theologica*, I, 2, 3[2]

The existence of God can be proved in five ways.

The first and more manifest way is the argument from motion. It is certain, and evident to our senses, that in the world some things are in motion. Now whatever is moved is moved by another, for nothing can be moved except it is in potentiality to that towards which it is moved; whereas a thing moves inasmuch as it is in act. For motion is nothing else than the reduction of something from potentiality to actuality. But nothing can be reduced from potentiality to actuality, except by something in a state of actuality. Thus that which is actually hot, as fire, makes wood, which is potentially hot, to be actually hot, and thereby moves and changes it. Now it is not possible that the same thing should be at once in actuality and potentiality in the same respect, but only in different respects. For what is actually hot cannot simultaneously be potentially hot; but it is simultaneously potentially cold. It is therefore impossible that in the same respect and in the same way a thing should be both mover and moved, i.e., that it should move itself. Therefore, whatever is moved must be moved by another. If that by which it is moved be itself moved, then this also must need be moved by another, and that by another again. But this cannot go on to infinity, because then there would be no first mover, and, consequently, no other mover, seeing that subsequent movers move only inasmuch as they are moved by the first mover; as the staff moves only because it is moved by the hand. Therefore it is necessary to arrive at a first mover, moved by no other; and this everyone understands to be God.

The second way is from the nature of efficient cause. In the world of sensible things we find there is an order of efficient causes. There is no case known (neither is it, indeed, possible) in which a thing is found to be the efficient cause of itself; for so it would be prior to itself, which is impossible. Now in efficient causes it is not possible to go on to infinity, because in all efficient causes following in order, the first is the cause of the intermediate cause, and the intermediate is the cause of the ultimate cause, whether the intermediate cause be several, or one only. Now to take away the cause is to take away the effect. Therefore, if there be no first cause among efficient causes, there will be no ultimate, nor any intermediate, cause. But if in efficient causes it is possible to go on to infinity, there will be no first efficient cause, neither will there be an ultimate effect, nor any intermediate efficient causes; all of which is plainly false. Therefore it is necessary to admit a first efficient cause, to which everyone gives the name of God.

The third way is taken from possibility and necessity, and runs thus. We find in nature things that are possible to be and not to be, since they are found to be generated, and to be corrupted, and consequently, it is possible for them to be and not to be. But it is impossible for these always to exist, for that which can not-be at some time is not. Therefore, if anything can not-be, then at one time there was nothing in existence. Now if this were true, even now there would be nothing in existence, because that which does not exist begins to exist only through something already existing. Therefore, if at one time nothing was in existence, it would have been impossible for anything to have begun to exist; and thus even now nothing would be in existence—which is absurd. Therefore, not all beings are merely possible, but there must exist something the existence of which is necessary. But every necessary thing either has its necessity caused by another, or not. Now it is impossible to go on to infinity in necessary things which have their necessity caused by another, as has been already proved in regard to efficient causes. Therefore we cannot but admit the existence of some being having of itself its own necessity, and not receiving it from another, but rather causing in others their necessity. This all men speak of as God.

The fourth way is taken from the gradation to be found in things. Among beings there are some more and some less good, true, noble, and the like. But *more* and *less* are predicated of different things according as they resemble in their different ways something which is the maximum, as a thing is said to be hotter according as it more nearly resembles that which is hottest; so that there is something which is truest, something best, something noblest, and, consequently, something which is most being, for those things that are greatest in truth are greatest in being, as it is written in *Metaph*. ii.[3] Now the maximum in any genus is the cause of all in that genus, as fire, which is the maximum of heat, is the cause of all hot things, as is said in the same book.[4] Therefore there must be something which is to all beings the cause of their being, goodness, and every other perfection; and this we call God.

The fifth way is taken from the governance of the world. We see that things which lack knowledge, such as natural bodies, act for an end, and this is evident from their acting always, or nearly always, in the same way, so as to obtain the best result. Hence it is plain that they achieve their end, not fortuitously, but designedly. Now whatever lacks knowledge cannot move towards an end, unless it be directed by some being endowed with knowledge and intelligence; as the arrow is directed by the archer. Therefore some intelligent being exists by whom all natural things are directed to their end; and this being we call God.

4
Summa Theologica, I, 3, 4

God is not only His own essence, as has been shown, but also His own being (*esse*). This may be shown in several ways. First, whatever a thing has besides its essence must be caused either by the constituent principles of that essence...or by some exterior agent....Therefore, if the being (*esse*) of a thing differs from its essence, this being (*esse*) must be caused either by some exterior agent or by the essential principles of the thing itself. Now it is impossible for a thing's being (*esse*) to be caused only by its essential constituent principles, for nothing can be the sufficient cause of its own being, if its being (*esse*) is caused. Therefore, that thing, whose being (*esse*) differs from its essence, must have its being caused by another. But this cannot be said of God, because we call God the first efficient cause. Therefore it is impossible that in God His being (*esse*) should differ from His essence.

Second, being (*esse*) is the actuality of every form or nature; for goodness and humanity are spoken of as actual, only because they are spoken of as being. Therefore, being (*esse*) must be compared to essence, if the latter is distinct from it, as actuality to potentiality. Therefore, since in God there is no potentiality, as shown above, it follows that in Him essence does not differ from being (*esse*). Therefore His essence is His being (*esse*).

Third...that which has being (*esse*), but is not being *(esse)*, is a being by participation. But God is His own essence, as was shown above. If, therefore, He is not His own being (*esse*), He will be not essential, but participated, being. He will not therefore be the first being—which is absurd. Therefore, God is His own being (*esse*), and not merely His own essence.

5
Summa Theologica, I, 4, 2

All the perfections of all beings are in God....First, because...it is plain that the effect pre-exists virtually in the efficient cause; and although to pre-exist in the potentiality of a material cause is to pre-exist in a more imperfect way, since matter as such is imperfect, and an agent as such is perfect, still to pre-exist virtually in the efficient cause is to pre-exist not in a more imperfect, but in a more perfect, way. Since therefore God is the first producing cause of things, the perfections of all things must pre-exist in God in a more eminent way. Dionysius touches upon this argument by saying of God: *It is not that He is this and not that, but that He is all, as the cause of all.*[5]

Secondly...God is being (*esse*) itself, of itself subsisted. Consequently, He must contain within Himself the whole perfection of being (*totam perfectionem essendi*). For it is clear that...if heat were self-subsisting, nothing of the virtue of heat would be wanting to it. Since therefore God is subsisting being (*esse*) itself, nothing of the perfection of being (*esse*) can be wanting to Him. Now all the perfections of all things pertain to the perfection of being (*esse*); for things are perfect precisely so far as they have being (*esse*) after some fashion. It follows therefore that the perfection of no thing is wanting to God. This line of argument, too, is touched upon by Dionysius when he says that *God exists not in any single mode, but embraces all being within Himself, absolutely, without limitation, uniformly;*[6] and afterwards he adds that *He is very being to subsisting things.*[7]

6
Summa Theologica, I, 14, 5

God necessarily knows things other than Himself. For it is manifest that He perfectly understands Himself; otherwise His being would not be perfect, since His being is His act of understanding. Now if anything is perfectly known, it follows of necessity that its power is perfectly known. But the power of anything can be perfectly known only by knowing to what that power extends. Since, therefore, the divine power extends to other things by the very fact that it is the first effective cause of all things, God must necessarily know things other than Himself.

And this appears still more plainly if we add that the very being (*esse*) of the first efficient cause—viz., God—is His own act of understanding. Hence whatever effects pre-exist in God, as in the first cause, must be in His act of understanding, and they must be there in an intelligible way: for everything which is in another is in it according to the mode of that in which it is.

Now in order to know how God knows things other than Himself, we must consider that a thing is known in two ways: in itself, and in another. A thing is known *in itself* when it is known by the proper species adequate to the knowable object itself; as when the eye sees a man through the species of a man. A thing is seen *in another* through the species of that which contains it; as when a part is seen in the whole through the species of the whole, or when a man is seen in a mirror through the species of the mirror, or by any other way by which one thing is seen in another.

So we say that God sees Himself in Himself, because He sees Himself through His essence; and He sees other things, not in themselves, but in Himself, inasmuch as His essence contains the likeness of things other than Himself.

7
Summa Theologica, I, 14, 6

It was shown above that whatever perfection exists in any creature wholly pre-exists and is contained in God in an excelling manner. Now not only what is common to creatures—viz., being—belongs to their perfection, but also what makes them distinguished from each other; as living and understanding, and the like, whereby living beings are distinguished from the non-living, and the intelligent from the non-intelligent. Likewise, every form whereby each thing is constituted in its own species is a perfection. Hence it is that all things pre-exist in God, not only as regards what is common to all, but also as regards what distinguishes one thing from another. And therefore as God contains all perfections in Himself, the essence of God is compared to all other essences of things, not as the common to the proper...but as perfect acts to imperfect....Now it is manifest that by a perfect act imperfect acts can be known not only in general but also by proper knowledge....

Since therefore the essence of God contains in itself all the perfection contained in the essence of any other being, and far more, God can know all things in Himself with a proper knowledge. For the nature proper to each thing consists in some particular participation of the divine perfection. Now God could not be said to know Himself perfectly unless He knew all the ways in which His own perfection can be shared by others. Neither could He know the very nature of being perfectly, unless He knew all the ways of being. Hence it is manifest that God knows all things with a proper knowledge, according as they are distinguished from each other.

8
Summa Theologica, I, 18, 4, *corp.*; *ad* 1 et *ad* 3

In God to live is to understand, as was before stated. But in God intellect, the thing understood, and the act of understanding are one and the same. Hence whatever is in God as understood is the very living or life of God. Now, therefore, since all things that have been made by God are in Him as things understood, it follows that all things in Him are the divine life itself.

Reply Obj. 1. Creatures are said to be in God in a two-fold sense. In one way, so far as they are contained and preserved by the divine power; even as we say that things that are in our power are in us. And thus creatures are said to be in God, even according to their existence in their own natures. In this sense we must understand the words of the Apostle when he says, *In Him we live, and move, and are*; since our living, being, and moving are themselves caused by God. In another sense, things are said to be in God as in Him who knows them; in which sense they are in God through their proper likenesses, which are nothing other in God than the divine essence. Hence things as they are in this way in God are the divine essence. And since the divine essence is life but not movement, it follows that things existing in God in this manner are not movement, but life.

Reply Obj. 3. If form only, and not matter, belonged to natural things, then in all respects natural things would exist more truly in the divine mind, by the ideas of them, than in themselves. For which reason, in fact, Plato held that the *separate* man was the true man, and that man, as he exists in matter, is man only by participation. But since matter enters into the being of natural things, we must say that natural things have a truer being (*esse*) absolutely in the divine mind than in themselves, because in that mind they have an uncreated being (*esse*), but in themselves a created being (*esse*). But to be this particular being, namely, a man or a horse, this they have more truly in their own nature than in the divine mind, because it belongs to human nature to be material, which, as existing in the divine mind, it is not. Even so a house has nobler being (*esse*) in the architect's mind than in matter; yet a material house is called a house more truly than the one which exists in the mind, since the former is actual, the latter only potential.

9
Summa Theologica, I, 12, 1

Some held that no created intellect can see the essence of God. This opinion, however, is not tenable.

For the ultimate beatitude of man consists in the use of his highest function, which is the operation of the intellect. Hence, if we suppose that a created intellect could never see God, it would either never attain to beatitude, or its beatitude would consist in something else beside God; which is opposed to faith. For the ultimate perfection of the rational creature is to be found in that which is the source of its being; since a thing is perfect so far as it attains to its source.

Further, the same opinion is also against reason. For there resides in every man a natural desire to know the cause of any effect which he sees. Thence arises wonder in men. But if the intellect of the rational creature could not attain to the first cause of things, the natural desire would remain vain.

Hence it must be granted absolutely that the blessed see the essence of God.

10
Summa Theologica, I, 12, 4

It is impossible for any created intellect to see the essence of God by its own natural power. For knowledge takes place according as the thing known is in the knower. But the thing known is in the knower according to the mode of the knower. Hence the knowledge of every knower is according to the mode of its own nature. If therefore the mode of being of a given thing exceeds the mode of the knower, it must result that the knowledge of that thing is above the nature of the knower.

It follows, therefore, that to know self-subsistent being (*ipsum esse subsistens*) is natural to the divine intellect alone, and that it is beyond the natural power of any created intellect; for no creature is its own being (*esse*), since its being (*esse*) is participated.

Therefore, a created intellect cannot see the essence of God unless God by His grace unites Himself to the created intellect, as an object made intelligible to it.

NOTES

1. From *The Principal Upanishads*, edited by S. Radhakrishnan (London: Allen and Unwin, 1953).

2. From *Basic Writings of St. Thomas Aquinas*, edited by Anton C. Pegis (New York: Random House, 1945).

3. *Metaph.*, Ia. 1 (993b 30).

4. Ibid., (993b 25).

5. *De Div. Nom.*, V, 8 (PG 3, 824).

6. Ibid., V, 4 (PG 3, 817).

7. Ibid.